# Old Wives' Lore

*For Isley the cat*

# OLD WIVES' LORE

## A Book of Old-Fashioned Tips & Remedies

## POLLY BLOOM

Michael O'Mara Books Limited

This paperback edition first published in 2016

First published in Great Britain in 2013 by
Michael O'Mara Books Limited
9 Lion Yard
Tremadoc Road
London SW4 7NQ

A CIP catalogue record for this book is available from the British
Library.

Papers used by Michael O'Mara Books Limited are natural, recyclable
products made from wood grown in sustainable forests. The
manufacturing processes conform to the environmental regulations of
the country of origin.

ISBN: 978-1-78243-517-4 in paperback print format
ISBN: 978-1-78243-162-6 in e-book format

1 2 3 4 5 6 7 8 9 10

www.mombooks.com

Illustrations by Thomas Bewick, except those on pages 187, 193 and 204,
which are Dover illustrations

Designed and typeset by K DESIGN, Winscombe, Somerset

Printed and bound by CPI Group (UK) Ltd, Croydon, CR0 4YY

# CONTENTS

**Part Two: Remedies for Home and Garden**

# INTRODUCTION: A VERY BRIEF HISTORY OF OLD WIVES' LORE

The terms 'old wives' tale' and 'old wives' lore' have curious associations and seem oddly anachronistic in the modern age. We think of the strange superstitions of the past and images abound in folklore and fiction of the weird woman living alone in the hut in the woods, cooking up her potions and casting her spells, or the crazy grandmother with her old-fashioned remedies and arcane advice. In a politically correct sense, the terms seem to be disparaging and denigrating, suggesting silly superstitions passed down through the generations that modern science can conclusively disprove and debunk. How many times have we heard somebody pass on a piece of esoteric and left-field advice only for it to be countered with the dismissive response: 'But that is just an old wives' tale, surely?' And yet, the phrase remains firmly entrenched in contemporary idiom and 'old wives' tales' have survived the centuries despite our scepticism.

So from where did the term originate? Well, variations can be found in the writings of ancient Greece, most notably in Plato's *Republic*, which discusses in part the nature of knowledge and the responsibilities involved in passing knowledge on to future generations. The Bible also mentions 'old wives' fables', but in a far less flattering light:

> *But refuse profane and old wives' fables, and exercise thyself rather unto godliness.*
>
> *Timothy 4:7 King James Bible*

There is a clear emphasis here on decrying myths and superstitions that are not intrinsically related to the word of God and rejecting pagan beliefs and ideas. Perhaps the notion that to believe in old wives' lore was somehow to be ungodly or blasphemous has filtered

down through the centuries and contributed to the cynicism often associated with seemingly old-fashioned wisdom, despite the secularization of Western society.

However, one of the first recorded publications of old wives' lore predates the *King James Bible* by over a century. *The Gospelles of Dystaues* or *The Distaff Gospels* is a medieval manuscript written in France around 1470 and translated into English and published by editor Wynkyn de Worde in 1507. De Worde was an associate of William Caxton and credited with furthering Caxton's work in modernizing the printing press in England and the first person to set up a press on London's now famous Fleet Street. *The Distaff Gospels* is comprised of over 250 different pieces of homespun advice and popular superstitions – the 'gospels' of the title. Each gospel is framed within a narrative of a collection of French peasant women who meet over a period of six nights to spin yarn at their distaffs and exchange their life experiences. Each member of the group presents her gospels in turn to the rest in the form of advice and opinions on everything from how to stop their husband's eye from wandering, to tips on household management, recipes, predicting the weather and old-fashioned superstitions. At the end of each presentation, another member of the group is invited to comment or add to the gospels that have been presented.

*The Distaff Gospels*, taken as a whole, paints a fascinating picture of peasant life in rural Europe in the fifteenth century; everyday practices, observations and beliefs. Many of the pieces of advice or old wives' lore still exist to this day, particularly superstitions concerning magpies and swans and ways of predicting the weather. Although some of the advice exchanged may seem quaintly bizarre and absurd to modern ears, the general impression created is of the methods and processes by which the women made sense of their world and how this 'knowledge' could be used principally to live and survive on a day-to-day basis. The fact that the *gospels* were imparted orally suggests a tradition of such meetings of old wives exchanging their tips and advice, which was then in turn passed down through the generations. If it was good enough for the old wives of *The Distaff Gospels* in the fifteenth century – who faced far greater hardships and perils than we do today – why shouldn't (within reason) old-fashioned home-spun advice and remedies be good enough (in certain circumstances) today?

Throughout history, as medical science has developed, there has been a tendency to dismiss old wives' lore. Interestingly though, the Victorian era, which witnessed great advances in medicine, also saw an explosion of books and other publications concerning home remedies and healing practices. It should be noted that there was no National Health Service in this period and although various health acts throughout the nineteenth century paved the way for the establishment of the NHS, death rates soared during the industrial revolution. It could be argued, then, that the poor, particularly in urban areas, were forced increasingly to rely upon home remedies for maintenance of health and well-being; old-fashioned wisdom that had been passed down to them on how best to treat various ailments. A good many of these old-fashioned remedies involved using materials that were close to hand or cheap and easily available – plants and herbs that could be found growing wild or were inexpensive and plentiful. A century or so on and there has been an upsurge in interest in herbal remedies, with thousands of websites devoted to how to treat most minor irritations and afflictions without recourse to costly trips to the local pharmacy.

This book is divided into two sections: remedies for health and well-being, and remedies for home and garden. The first of these concerns common minor ailments and irritations, from stomach bugs and colds, to arthritis and hayfever. The remedies, as a rule, use things easy to hand that can be found in most households. While every care has been taken to research their efficacy and avoid toxic or harmful substances, it goes without saying that these remedies are in no sense designed to substitute professional medical advice. They are suggestions for old-fashioned treatments and not intended as a course of medicinal action that will guarantee a cure or significant results.

To eliminate any doubt or concern about any possible side effects or allergic reactions, it is advisable to contact a medical professional before attempting any of the remedies outlined.

The second section of the book is concerned with gardening tips and household management. Gardeners' lore is steeped in old-fashioned methods and practices with a wealth of literature on the subject. Gardening has become increasingly popular in recent decades with many thousands of people taking it up as a hobby either by getting involved in community projects or acquiring allotments to grow their own fruit and vegetables. Similar to the first section though, although the advice and tips are based on tried and tested common sense, they are not guaranteed to always solve the problem they address and any number of factors can contribute to a crop of vegetables failing or plants dying.

The intention of this book, then, is to provide some suggestions, based on time-honoured remedies passed down, on how to approach certain everyday problems. Some of them may work, others may not, but in the spirit of the old wives, it is in my opinion worth giving some of them a try and finding out. I have endeavoured, where possible, to add some interesting trivia and titbits· of history, which I hope help to lighten things a little and provide some interest and entertainment but concede that subjects such as haemorrhoids and arthritis are no laughing matter to the afflicted. Most of all, I hope that readers will find, in whatever small way, something that is of use to them in their everyday life.

*Polly Bloom*

# ACKNOWLEDGEMENTS

I should like to thank the following people without whom this book would not have been possible: Toby Buchan and Anna Marx, my editors at Michael O'Mara Books, for getting the project off the ground and for their continued patient help and support; the design, production and marketing team at MOM; my good friend Joe Moorman, a master gardener, for his help and advice with gardeners' lore; Jane Taylor, Joanna Taylor, James Fleet and Lucas Rose for their help with research and additional material and suggestions; the staff of The University of Sussex Library and Hove Library for fielding my queries and the use of their facilities; and, last but not least, the support of all my family and friends.

# PART ONE

# Remedies for Health and Well-being

# SPOTS, WARTS, BOILS AND BLACKHEADS

An entire pharmaceutical sub-industry has sprung up around the curse of puberty: spots, boils and acne. Various face creams and ointments flood a market usually backed up by shrewd and often cynical advertising. In truth, regular facial cleansing with hot flannels and warm water allied to careful dietary monitoring can usually help to alleviate the awkwardness and embarrassment of adolescent skin complaints. Old-fashioned remedies also offer an alternative to expensive commercial skincare products and are very simple to prepare.

Baking powder (bicarbonate of soda) mixed with water into a paste and applied to the inflamed area twice daily is a common solution and one that is also recommended for mouth ulcers. Similar pastes and cleansers for the face can also be made by a variety of methods using easy-to-find ingredients:

❖ Gently cook a finely chopped onion in water with a large tablespoon of honey (dissolve the honey in the water before adding the onion). As the mixture starts to cool, mash into a paste with a fork and dab on to spots with cotton wool.

❖ Take a teacup and fill approximately one quarter with freshly grated horseradish (be careful when grating as the pungent vapours can irritate the eyes). Then fill up half the cup with honey, stir and leave for a day or two in a warm, dry place. Apply the resulting mixture to spots and boils two to three times a day.

❖ Bake a fresh fig in the oven and leave to cool until it can be handled easily. Cut the fig in half and scoop out the soft flesh into a clean bowl. Spread the mash on to a small sticking plaster or other dressing and leave on overnight. Replace with a clean dressing the following morning.

❖ Mix a teaspoonful of ground turmeric with coconut oil and use with cotton wool as a facial cleanser twice a day.

Warts held a peculiar place in old wives' lore, largely due to their association with witchcraft and the fairytale archetype of the warty old hag who resides in the cottage in the woods. Warts are created by the papilloma virus, which causes small, hard bumps to appear on the skin. Despite the folklore that sprang up around them, warts are generally quite harmless. It is the sudden appearance of these blemishes that most perplexed previous generations, leading to explanations ranging from accidental contact with frogs or toads to the first signs of the onset of insanity. No less bizarre were the methods deployed for removing the warts, from rubbing with a toad or tying horse hair around the fingers or toes on which the wart has appeared, to beheading a live eel and rubbing the blood into the area around the wart. The fact that warts will eventually disappear of their own accord as the human immune system breaks down the virus served to add to the validity of these macabre remedies. Most warts displaying troublesome longevity can usually be removed by modern medical methods such as surgery, freezing with liquid nitrogen or laser treatment, or by trying some of the natural remedies below that do not require a significant leap of faith.

❖ Take a banana skin and either wrap a piece of it around the wart (if the wart is on a finger or toe) and cover in a bandage, or rub the wart gently with it several times a day. If using the bandage method, change the banana skin dressing each day and apply the pithy inside part of the skin, not the waxy exterior.

❖ Apply castor oil directly to the wart by dabbing either with cotton wool or a soft, clean cloth or, alternatively, soak a ball of cotton wool in castor oil and stick over the wart with a plaster.

❖ Make a sticking plaster out of duct tape and cover the wart for about a week. Remove the duct tape plaster by soaking it in warm, soapy water and then scrub the wart with a pumice stone – the wart should just fall off; if not, repeat the process for another week.

Scientific research has proven the duct tape/pumice stone method to be extremely effective, although the reasons for this are unclear. It seems probable that one of the chemicals used in the production of commercial duct tape, such as zinc oxide or powdered aluminium, is particularly effective at breaking down the papilloma virus that causes warts to appear.

# SUPERSTITIONS AND HOKUM:
## Boils And The
## Black Death

Many old wives' superstitions concerning boils have a strong association with death. This is probably as a result of the great plague, the fourteenth-century pandemic thought to have claimed the lives of between forty and sixty per cent of the population of Europe. The most common symptom of the black death was the sudden swelling up of large boils and pustules known as 'buboes', which the Italian renaissance writer Boccaccio described in his classic text *The Decameron* as growing to the size of 'common apples'. Although most victims of the Black Death died within two to seven days of becoming infected, some bizarre 'cures' were tried, largely through desperation. Some of the more colourful remedies included shaving a live chicken and tying it under the armpits or to the groin region (where the buboes often first appeared), or pulping frogs and rubbing the resulting slime into the infected areas.

There are two surviving old wives' superstitions from the West Country region of England, which were recommended for boils in printed materials up until the 1950s. The first concerns placing a poultice of strong-smelling herbs on to boils for at least two days and then tying the poultice rags to the coffin of a recently deceased person just prior to burial. The second remedy, possibly even more bizarre, states that to cure boils, a friend or relative of the person with boils should dance six times around a recently dug grave in the dead of night; however, this should only be done when the moon is covered by clouds.

# ARTHRITIS, ACHES AND PAINS AND GOUT

Although it will be of scant comfort to the millions of people around the world who suffer from any of the variant forms of arthritis, this most discomforting and persistent of afflictions has plagued human beings since ancient times. One of the oldest surviving medical dictionaries is contained on the Ebers Papyrus, believed to have been written around 1550 BC. Written in Hieratic Egyptian on to a twenty-metre-long scroll, the Ebers Papyrus outlines a series of medical complaints and treatments, among them an ailment remarkably similar to rheumatoid arthritis.

Legendary Greek physician Hippocrates (*c.* 460– *c.* 370 BC), of the Hippocratic Oath, wrote extensively about inflammation of the joints but didn't distinguish between its different forms, apart from gout – which he termed 'podagra' or 'foot-trap'. Interestingly, Hippocrates makes a class distinction between gout and other forms of arthritis, noting that 'podagra' was more likely to affect people who led indulgent and decadent lifestyles (the upper classes), whereas other forms of arthritis were more prevalent in artisan workers and the lower classes. The Greco-Roman physician Galen (AD 129–216) is believed to be the first person to coin the term *rheumatismus* or rheumatism, taken from the Greek word *rheum*, meaning 'flux', and relating to congested humours (the ancient Greek physicians, taking their cue from Hippocrates, believed all human ailments came from imbalances in the 'humours' – fluids that inhabit the body).

Among the many remedies prescribed by the classical physicians, ranging from burning and inhaling sandalwood incense, to sacrificing lame horses on temple alters, the most effective seem to be the use of frankincense and myrrh. Yes, two parts of the triumvirate of gifts bestowed upon the baby Jesus in the Bible.

Frankincense is the common term for resin extracted from the Boswellia tree that grows in North

Africa and parts of India. Frankincense has long had a varied list of medical and non-medical uses, including as sacred incense burned in religious ceremonies, as a key component of Arabic perfumes and as a form of chewing gum taken as a digestive aid. Recent medical trials undertaken by several universities around the world have unveiled startling results concerning the all-round medicinal properties of frankincense. Cardiff University Medical School, in particular, has trialled the use of frankincense on patients suffering from osteoarthritis and chronic inflammation of the joints and report around a seventy per cent improvement in swelling and a considerable increase in joint mobility. The Cardiff scientists believe frankincense contains an active agent that inhibits the production of key inflammatory molecules and helps prevent the breakdown of the cartilage tissue that causes arthritis.

Frankincense creams are available to purchase online and from specialist aromatherapists, and it seems likely that if additional medical research backs up the findings of Cardiff University and others, commercial creams will soon be freely available. However, until that time, frankincense is freely available as an essential oil, which can be gently applied to the inflamed joints, and in capsule form as a health supplement.

Myrrh, in contrast, has long been recognized as an anti-inflammatory, antiseptic medicine and was often used by surgeons to dress battle wounds in ancient times (see Cuts and Grazes). Myrrh essential oil can be used in the same way as frankincense, and there are also frankincense and myrrh combined creams available on the market. Myrrh is much cheaper and more economical if bought in bulk in resin form and overleaf is a simple recipe for making your own myrrh salve, which also doubles as an antiseptic for cuts and grazes.

# MYRRH SALVE

## *Ingredients:*

50 g (1.8 oz) myrrh resin
olive oil
several tablespoons of beeswax

## *Method:*

❖ Take the myrrh resin and roughly crush into a loose (but not fine) powder with a pestle and mortar.

❖ Grease the base of a large cooking pot with olive oil, spoon in the myrrh powder and cover with around an inch (2.5 cm) of oil.

❖ Gently heat the oil on a low temperature for two to three hours to infuse the oil with the myrrh.

❖ Add the beeswax to the mixture and continue to heat and stir until the beeswax has dissolved. Allow to cool.

❖ Spoon the mixture into airtight containers and place somewhere cool and dry to set.

A less exotic (or biblical) herbal remedy from old wives' lore concerns the use of mustard seeds to counteract arthritis and aching joints. Mustard seeds contain selenium and magnesium, both of which have anti-inflammatory effects, and the use of mustard seed plasters or poultices has been common practice in rural areas for centuries.

## MUSTARD SEED POULTICE

### *Ingredients:*

white or brown mustard seeds
vinegar
wheat flour
cold water

### *Equipment:*

pestle and mortar or seed grinder
muslin cloth

# *Method:*

❖ Crush the seeds of white or brown mustard into a powder using a pestle and mortar or seed grinder.

❖ In a bowl, moisten the powder with a little vinegar, then sprinkle with wheat flour (roughly an amount equivalent to the mustard seed powder).

❖ Add cold water a little at a time and mix into a thick, gloopy paste.

❖ Spread the mixture on a strip of muslin cloth and cover with another strip of cloth to make a mustard paste sandwich.

❖ Place the cloth on the inflamed area and press down lightly for about twenty minutes. Remove if the poultice becomes too uncomfortable.

❖ After removing the poultice, gently wash the affected area with warm water.

Gout is sometimes referred to as 'the disease of kings', probably on account of historical records showing that both Alexander the Great and Henry VIII suffered from the affliction. Gout is a type of arthritis that is caused by the accumulation of uric acid in the body. Crystals of uric acid can form in a joint and this can lead to intense pain and inflammation. While gout is classically thought of as a condition which affects the feet and particularly the toes, in fact, a build-up of uric acid crystals can occur anywhere in the joints, including the knees, ankles, wrists and hands. Gout, although painful, usually subsides after a while and can be effectively controlled by careful diet considerations (too much red meat, dairy products and red wine exacerbates gout).

However, certain old wives' remedies prevail, the most common of which is to eat fresh cherries when they are in season. There is some medical proof for the efficacy of cherries in that they are rich in proanthocyanidins, which help to neutralize uric acid and have anti-inflammatory properties. The eating of globe artichokes or the making of hot poultices from boiled artichoke leaves is also recommended by some herbalists, although there is scant medical proof that this actually works – eating fresh fruit and vegetables is good for us anyway. One old wives' tale that is definitely untrue is that eating too many strawberries causes gout; in fact, strawberries, like cherries, are a useful antidote.

# Gout And The Boston Tea Party

Gout had a curious part to play in American history and the American Revolution. British statesman William Pitt The Elder was an outspoken opponent of levying taxation on the British colonies, as he saw this as unconstitutional unless ratified by the colonies' elected representatives. Pitt suffered from chronic gout-related arthritis and was regularly absent from Parliament. It was during one of his prolonged absences that the controversial Stamp Act of 1765 was passed. Upon recovering from his gout, Pitt succeeded in getting the Act repealed, with the famous words, 'The Americans are the sons, not the bastards, of England. As subjects, they are entitled to the right of common representation and cannot be bound to pay taxes without their consent.'

However, it wasn't long before Pitt

succumbed to gout again and during his second lengthy absence, Lord Townshend persuaded Parliament to levy a heavy duty on colonial imports of tea with the Tea Act of 1773, which caused the Boston Tea Party and the ensuing American War of Independence.

In a further gout-related twist, when the committee of five was formed in 1776 to draft the Declaration of Independence and present it to Congress, key member Benjamin Franklin was forced to miss most of the meetings due to succumbing to 'the disease of kings'.

# CUTS AND GRAZES

Most of us, from time to time, bemoan our 'health and safety gone mad culture' despite being fortunate enough to live in a relatively accident-free work and home environment, unlike our predecessors. That said, we all still occasionally suffer from unavoidable cuts and grazes, and have access to professional treatment for the more serious of these injuries.

For our ancestors, life expectancy among the poor was low, averaging forty, and even a relatively small cut on a healthy individual could prove fatal if it became infected. Often bizarre and painful methods were employed to try to limit infection, for example: applying animal urine; branding deep cuts, thus cauterizing them to reduce the chance of external infection; or, in medieval times, encouraging a deep cut to heal by allowing ants to feed on the edge of the wound.

In battle, cuts inflicted by swords and daggers were often treated with alcohol, which did kill germs to some extent, but probably as many men died from infection as did from the actual injuries. During the Middle Ages, villagers were usually tended by a local woman who would have her own preferred treatments for cuts, depending on what herbs and spices were available locally, and which had been passed down through generations. Some of these traditional remedies can still be used today for minor cuts and grazes. Below are some of the more harmless remedies:

❖ Boil lavender flowers in a little water, strain and allow to cool to a tolerable temperature before applying directly to the area.

❖ After cleaning the wound with water, apply a dressing coated with honey, which has antiseptic qualities.

❖ Sprinkle brown sugar onto a clean cut and rub some petroleum jelly around the edge before applying a dry dressing.

* Lemon juice dripped onto a cut will stop the bleeding (it will also sting!).

* Sprinkle turmeric powder onto a clean wound to stem bleeding.

* Place one or two bruised geranium flowers onto a graze to encourage it to scab over quickly.

# Natural Victorian Cure for Wounds, Cuts and Abrasions (1890)

[*Not recommended!*]

The best simple remedy for surface wounds, such as cuts, abrasion of the skin, etc., is charcoal. Take a large coal from the fire, pulverize it, apply it to the wound, and cover the whole with a rag. The charcoal absorbs the fluid secreted by the wound, and lays the foundation of the scab; it also prevents the rag from irritating the flesh, and is an antiseptic. Without waiting for it to stop bleeding, press the edges of the lacerated flesh together, and apply immediately a plaster made of soot and cream, binding it firmly on. This is not to be removed until healed.

When a nail or pin has been run into the foot, instantly bind on a rind of salt pork, and keep quiet till the wound is well. The lockjaw is often caused by such wounds, if neglected.

# STINGS, SKIN IRRITATION AND INSECT BITES

When Aristotle (384–322 BC) asserted that 'one swallow does not a summer make, nor one fine day', he was describing the transient nature of personal happiness and contentment. In a literal sense, to spot one swallow returning from winter migration is actually a pretty good indication that summer is on the way. On the other hand, to wake up one morning and find that mosquitoes and other blood-sucking beasties have been gleefully feeding on you during the night is a sure-fire sign that summer is up and running. Mosquitoes, midges, gnats and (especially) wasps are the pests of the summertime, intent on spoiling everybody's fun. Pharmaceutical companies produce a variety of different deterrents and barrier creams designed to repel insects and treat bites and stings with, on balance, a fair-to-middling amount of success. They are resourceful though, these mini-mites, as the seemingly inexorable quest to stamp out malaria has proved. Over time, it seems, insects start to become immune to the chemical deterrents put in their path. So what did the old wives do regarding the prevention and treatment of insect bites and stings?

Bee stings differ from wasp stings in that bees, on account of it proving fatal to them, will generally avoid stinging humans. Wasps, on the other hand, seem to sting just for the hell of it. The first thing to do when stung by a bee is remove the sting immediately. This can be done with tweezers or be plucked out with fingernails (it won't sting again). The longer bee stings are allowed to remain in the body, the more severe the reaction will be. One old-fashioned way to soothe bee stings is to apply the cut surface of an onion to the spot. Fresh-cut onions contain enzymes that break down prostaglandins, the lipid compounds that regulate the body and its response to injuries, which cause pain and swelling. The juice of a fresh onion helps to minimize the swelling and provide a mild anaesthetic. A peeled and cut clove of garlic will also perform the same trick.

Another old wives' remedy was to brew a pot of strong herbal tea using either (preferably) fresh or dried thyme or parsley. Once brewed, leave to cool for a few minutes to aid the infusion of the herbs and then dab the sting with clean, sterilized cotton wool. Dried parsley can also be mixed into a paste with a little hot water and applied as a poultice to insect bites and stings. Other simple remedies include making a bandage out of banana skins and wrapping it around the bite, pressing the pith side against the bite or sting and squeezing fresh lemon juice onto the infected area.

Although the above remedies help to relieve soreness and irritation from insect bites and stings, it is better to avoid being bitten or stung in the first place. As mentioned above, there are a variety of insect repellent sprays and creams commercially available, which vary in effectiveness from person to person. One substance that the old wives swear by, though, is apple cider vinegar, which can be used as an insect repellent in a variety of ways. The simplest way is to ingest four large spoonfuls after breakfast. For those with an aversion to sour and acidic flavours, the vinegar can be diluted with water if necessary. Insects in general, and female mosquitoes in particular (who precipitate the spread of diseases such as malaria and the West Nile Virus), hate vinegar. There is also an age-old recipe for vinegar-based insect repellent that reputedly dates back to the Black Death pandemic that ravaged Europe in the mid fourteenth century. With an estimated two million people succumbing to the plague in a little over two years, the Black Death provided rich, if precarious, pickings for thieves and criminals. According to legend, thieves and burglars would bathe in a mixture of vinegar and herbs before heading out to steal from the dead, as the smell of the vinegar deterred the microscopic rat fleas that carried the deadly virus from biting them. Here is the recipe and method for the insect repellent, which, if it was effective during one of the worst pandemics in human history, is certainly worth giving a try today.

# BLACK DEATH INSECT REPELLENT

## *Ingredients:*

1 litre of apple cider vinegar
4 heaped tbsp each of dried sage, rosemary, lavender,
thyme and mint

## *Equipment:*

stainless-steel saucepan
funnel with filter papers
large airtight glass demijohn.

## *Method:*

❧ Pour the vinegar and three tablespoons of each
herb into a saucepan and heat gently for twenty
minutes, stirring regularly (do not boil, as this
impairs the active ingredients). Allow to cool.

❧ Once cooled, pour contents of saucepan into a
sterilized demijohn, scrape in any of the sludge

of herbs from the bottom of the pan and add one more tablespoon of each herb to the mix.

✤ Seal tightly and store in a warm, dry place for two to three weeks, shaking the demijohn vigorously at least twice a day to agitate the mix.

✤ After two to three weeks, filter out the herbs using a funnel and filter paper (this can be quite fiddly and time-consuming). Wash and sterilize the demijohn and then pour the filtered, herb-infused vinegar back into the jar.

To use the above repellent as a spray, simply fill a spray bottle with a nozzle half full of the vinegar and dilute with sterilized water, and spray directly onto the skin. If the mild vinegary odour is not to your liking, add some essential oils (a few drops) such as citronella or lavender to the spray bottle and shake gently.

The old wives also recommended eating a few cloves of raw garlic as a powerful insect deterrent, as garlic sweats out through the skin and mosquitoes are primarily attracted by odours produced by the sweat glands. The smell of garlic, however, is too pungent and over-powering for their sensors and acts to make the blood seem unattractive or contaminated (who would have thought mosquitoes were fussy about who they bite?). However, the smell of garlic is not to everyone's taste and may not make one particularly attractive to be around in social situations.

# COUGHS AND COLDS

On average, a reasonably healthy adult can expect to come down with a common cold at least four times a year. The severity of symptoms varies each time, partly because what we know as 'the common cold' can be caused by any one of two hundred different viruses. Classic symptoms include a sore throat, blocked sinuses, sneezing, running nose, tickly cough and mucus congestion on the chest.

There are many commercial cold medicines on the market, each claiming to provide fast relief from the troublesome effects, but most people can usually shake off a cold within a few days by drinking a lot of fluids, resting and taking vitamin C supplements. This has not dampened the market for non-prescription medicines, however, which is estimated to be worth over five hundred million dollars a year to the pharmaceutical industry in the United States alone.

The classic old wives' cure for the common cold is chicken broth. The beneficial effects of sipping hot soup – other than it being great comfort food – are twofold. First, it aids hydration, which is a key factor in recovery; and second, the steam from chicken soup helps relieve a congested nose and throat. Recent research has also suggested that chicken soup also reduces the inflammation associated with a cold by reducing the movement of white blood cells in the upper respiratory tract.

Hot lemon with honey is another time-honoured remedy for cold relief; the honey helps to soothe sore throats and the lemon juice provides much-needed shots of vitamin C to the body. Chewing horseradish is recommended to help relieve nasal congestion and mucus build-up on the chest. Simply cut small slices of horseradish and inhale deeply while chewing. Horseradish is something of an acquired taste, though, and another method for those with delicate palettes is to grate fresh horseradish into a cup, pour on hot water, stir and inhale the steam. Superfoods such as garlic and ginger are also effective cold remedies. Load up the chicken broth with plenty of crushed garlic and drink lots of ginger tea.

Cough syrups and tinctures date back to ancient times. The Edwin Smith Papyrus contains details of pharmacopoeia (medicine-making), which suggests the ancient Egyptians were making cough mixtures from peppermint and eucalyptus oils at least ten thousand years ago. Vodka was originally produced in Russia as a cough syrup to be diluted with water and gargled as early as the eighth century (vodka mixed with ground black pepper is the classic 'cure all' remedy in Russia to this day). Here are two simple recipes for making your own cough syrup.

# THYME COUGH SYRUP

## *Ingredients:*

boiled water
fresh thyme leaves
honey

## *Method:*

✤ Pour two mugs of recently boiled water over two tablespoons of fresh thyme leaves, and allow to brew until cooled to room temperature.

✤ Once cooled, filter out the thyme leaves through a strainer and stir in one cup of honey.

✤ The mixture can then be transferred to a suitable glass jar and kept in the fridge to be used as required (two tablespoons early in the morning and late at night are recommended).

# HONEY AND CLOVE SYRUP

## *Ingredients:*

5 whole cloves

honey

## *Method:*

❖ Place the cloves in a cup of honey and refrigerate for at least twenty-four hours.

❖ Take one or two teaspoons several times a day. The clove-infused honey helps soothe the throat and counteract soreness as the cloves act as a natural anaesthetic.

# Victorian Remedies for Coughs

Morphine was routinely used in Victorian remedies for coughs and colds, particularly in soothers for young children. As too was laudanum, which contains both morphine and codeine. Here are some Victorian recipes for different types of cough using various unusual ingredients. Even if you can get your hands on 'barberry bark', do not try them at home!

## General Cough

2 tablespoonfuls linseed, 4 oz liquorice root or Spanish juice, 4 oz elecampane root, 3 quarts water, boiled down to 3 pints. Dose: a wineglassful four or five times a day.

## General Cough, Another

1 drachm powder of tragacanth, 2 drachms syrup of white poppies, 40 drops laudanum, 4 oz water. Shake the powder in the water till it is dissolved, then add the others. Dose: a teaspoonful three times a day.

## Asthmatic Cough

2 good handfuls coltsfoot leaves, 1 oz garlic, 2 quarts water boiled down to 3 pints. Strain, add 8 oz sugar and boil gently for 10 minutes. Dose: half a cupful occasionally.

## Consumptive Cough

2 pennyworth each of sanctuary, horehound, barberry bark; 1 pennyworth each of agrimony, raspberry leaves, clevers and ground ivy; 4 oz extract of liquorice; ½ a teaspoonful of cayenne pepper. Gently simmer in 2 gallons of water for half an hour. Dose: half a cupful four times a day.

# HEAD LICE AND OTHER CRITTERS

Most parents have experienced that initial moment of horror when they first discover head lice in the hair of their treasured and scrupulously scrubbed offspring. High standards of personal hygiene do not appear to deter the insects and often what results is a seemingly endless cycle of reinfection as a child comes into daily contact with their peers at nursery or school.

Head lice are tiny insects that live in human hair. They use claws on the end of their legs to cling onto hair and feed by biting the scalp and drinking the blood. The white eggs laid by the female are called nits and are often easier to spot than the actual insect. Head lice cannot fly or jump, and therefore close contact is required in order for them to crawl from head to head. They cannot survive away from a human head for very long and, hence, you are unlikely to catch head lice from a pillow or towel.

In the past, head lice infestations seem to have been accepted as the norm and did not particularly worry people, as everyone carried a variety of parasites around with them, especially the poor. Interestingly, when Mary Queen of Scots returned to Scotland after living for years in France, she found it very disrespectful that men kept their hats on while sitting down to eat at banquets, until it was explained to her that they did this to stop head lice falling onto their food. This does invite the question: were the French more hygienic or less particular about what was on their plates?

Nowadays, a variety of chemical treatments for head lice can be purchased from the pharmacy but these can soon become a drain on the family budget, especially when there are regular outbreaks, and often, after repeated applications, head lice develop a resistance to the medication. Below are listed some natural and less costly remedies which work just as well:

❖ Coat the hair completely with mayonnaise before bedtime. Wear a plastic shower cap to protect bedding. In the morning, rinse out the mayonnaise with cider vinegar and then shampoo and condition as usual. Heat a metal nit comb in boiling water and then comb through the wet hair, thin sections at a time. Repeat the process twice more, leaving a day between each treatment.

❧ Massage tea tree oil into the hair and scalp. Put on a shower cap and leave for thirty minutes. Wash off with a mixture of shampoo and a few drops more of tea tree oil. (Do a skin test first, as some people can have a reaction to tea tree oil.)

❧ Soak the hair with beer. Again, don a shower cap and leave for thirty minutes. Rinse off the beer but do not use shampoo, then apply conditioner as usual. Comb wet hair through with a nit comb.

# Drastic Measures!

Extract from a 1914 Nursing Exam in England:

*Question*: If when visiting school children in their own homes you found a bad case of *pediculi capitis* [head lice], how would you proceed to deal with it?

*Answer*: Try and get the consent of the mother to have the child's head shaved, rub in paraffin all over the head, warn the mother to keep the child away from the fire or any light, cover the child's head up in a towel or a capulin, tell the mother to take it off in the morning and immediately burn it. Wash the child's head well with soft soap and water; continue the treatment until the head is clean. Advise the mother to wash the other children's heads with soft soap and water, and tooth-comb them daily with vinegar to be sure they are free from infection.

# Scabies

When I was a teenager and living with my grandmother, I contracted scabies. She was absolutely horrified, as she firmly believed in the myths surrounding this very itchy and unpleasant infestation, namely that it was exclusively a sexually transmitted disease and that you had to be dirty to get it. Happily, I did finally manage to convince her that my standards of hygiene had not inexplicably plummeted and that I had in fact picked up these nasty parasites from an old mattress I had slept on at a music festival.

Scabies is a contagious skin disease caused by tiny mites, which burrow into the skin where they lay their eggs and continue to multiply. Symptoms include itching, thin red lines on the skin, rashes, and sores that can become infected. It is possible to go as long as six weeks before even realizing that you have contracted scabies because the mites tend to seek out crevices in the body that provide them with warmth. The bugs cannot be seen by the human eye and the first signs of scabies often appear similar to pimples or mosquito bites.

The mites cannot jump – they have to crawl from person to person, and therefore close contact for a prolonged period is necessary for them to travel, so sexual intimacy can be a means of infection, as can hand-holding as opposed to a quick handshake. Whole families can therefore get infected and outbreaks of scabies can also occur in residential homes, nurseries or anywhere people are in regular close contact – anyone can get it. However, these parasites can survive away from a human host for about twenty-four to thirty-six hours, and thus sharing towels or bedding can facilitate transmission.

The first recorded reference to scabies is believed to be in the Bible, and later Aristotle described 'lice' that 'escape from little pimples if they are pricked', which is understood to be a reference to scabies.

As well as prescription creams, there are old-fashioned remedies for scabies, such as:

❖ Tea tree oil. Take a warm bath, in which you have added twenty to thirty drops of tea tree oil. Repeat this procedure several times a day, and it is claimed that this will eradicate the infestation.

✣ Sulphur. Soaps and creams containing sulphur have traditionally been used to kill the scabies mites. Most over-the-counter products contain six to ten per cent sulphur. Sulphur only kills adult mites, not their eggs, and therefore the soap or cream has to be used for several weeks to eliminate the infection. Caution should be taken when treating young children, as sulphur can sometimes irritate their skin.

These treatments have to be carried out for at least three weeks; all household members and close contacts should be treated at the same time – even if they have no sign of scabies, as the symptoms can take up to six weeks to materialize.

In conjunction with treating the condition, all bedding, towels and clothing should be machine washed at a high temperature. Carpets and soft furnishings should be thoroughly vacuumed.

# Tapeworms

Tapeworms normally live in animals, but can be passed on to humans through bad sanitation and also by consumption of raw meat. Although instances of people being inhabited by these parasites are extremely rare in developed countries, there are still some areas in remoter regions of the world where it is not uncommon. As opportunities for foreign travel to more exotic regions have grown in recent years, I thought it worth mentioning these rather alarming creatures that can grow up to thirty feet long in the intestine.

Most of us are aware of the countless 'miracle' diets, which regularly hit the news, claiming to be a quick fix for shedding excess pounds. However, this is not a recent phenomenon, as it was the Victorian age that saw the emergence of these fads, which gained popularity in affluent society, along with the stringing of tighter and tighter corsets. One of the craziest was the 'tapeworm diet', which involved swallowing a pill containing beef tapeworm cysts, the theory being that the parasite would reach maturity in the intestine and absorb ingested food. There was a resurgence of this supposed method of weight loss in the 1920s and, even today, despite being illegal, it is possible to purchase these dangerous tablets.

You may not be aware that you actually have this freeloader on board, as a tapeworm infection does not always carry any symptoms and can go unnoticed for several years, or can be mistaken for another illness, manifesting itself as stomach ache that may be

accompanied by sickness and diarrhoea. Often, the first indication of having a tapeworm is when segments of the worm break off and appear in your faeces.

Old remedies for tapeworm include:

❧ Starving the patient and then placing a piece of food in their mouth in order to tempt the parasite out.

❧ Sit the victim in a bath of milk, again with the idea of enticing the creature out and drowning it.

I would not actually recommend either of these as a means of dealing with the problem. There are homeopathic parasite cleansers available, but to be honest, I would suggest consulting a doctor if you suspect you have been invaded by something akin to a creature in the movie *Alien*.

# ANXIETY AND DEPRESSION

# Anxiety

Anxiety and stress have sometimes been described as a modern illness, brought about by the generally hectic lives we now lead compared to those of our ancestors. However, anxiety has always been a human condition; as Aesop (620–564 BC), the famous writer of fables, pointed out: 'A crust eaten in peace is better than a banquet partaken in anxiety.'

We have all experienced a degree of anxiety at one time or another, be it prior to a job interview, having to make an important decision, meeting new people, or when faced with a problem; however, some people live in a constant state of anxiety, which affects their ability to function in everyday life. Sufferers encounter feelings of being overwhelmed, often accompanied by a sense of loneliness and isolation. Signs of anxiety include:

❖ feelings of panic;

❖ difficulty concentrating;

❖ sleeping problems;

❖ shortness of breath;

❖ muscle tension;

❖ palpitations.

The subject feels unrealistic fear, worry and uneasiness, which is usually non-specific and unfocused. Anxiety is not the same as fear, which is brought on by a real threat of danger whether to oneself or a loved one.

As well as taking regular exercise, reducing alcohol and caffeine intake and stopping smoking, there are various counselling techniques that can help anxiety sufferers, including hypnosis. For those who do not want to go down the route of taking prescription drugs to aid the condition, here are a few traditional remedies:

❧ Lemon balm. This has been used for centuries to relieve stress and anxiety, help with sleeping and to lift the spirits. Drink a cup of lemon balm tea two or three times a day.

❧ Lavender oil. Place lavender oil on your pillow, clothing or handkerchief. Add lavender to a warm bath and soak to help to ease stress.

❧ Drink a cup of camomile tea a few times a day to relieve tension.

# Onions for Insomnia

Insomnia and anxiety often go hand in hand, with the one exacerbating the other. Orthodox medicine offers various solutions, including certain sedative drugs that may produce bad side effects. However, for many, the answer lies in the simple onion. Onions contain Riboflavin, also known as vitamin B2, which is vital in maintaining health in humans and animals, and thought to be deficient in those suffering from insomnia.

One Victorian remedy recommends stewing Spanish onions and eating a couple softened, as a syrup or as a soup, adding a little butter to taste. This should be done before bed.

If you can stomach it, try eating one bulb of raw onion before sleeping. If you can't stand the taste, simply sniffing in its pungent aromas ought to suffice. Warning: this may produce tears before bed!

# Depression

It is perfectly normal to experience low moods from time to time, often for no apparent reason, but when this feeling is prolonged the condition is classified as depression. Depression can be triggered by a variety of things, some of the commonest being: conflict with family members or friends; death or loss; serious illness; certain medications; past experiences of abuse; stress at work; or due to a history of depression in the family. Even positive events such as getting married or starting a new job can bring on an episode for some sufferers. Lack of sunshine can badly affect people who have Seasonal Affective Disorder (SAD), which is related to a change of season and is four times more common in women than in men. Some new mothers also experience post-natal depression.

It is estimated that approximately eight per cent of sufferers are not receiving treatment, possibly due to the perceived stigma associated with mental health problems. Women are twice as likely to suffer from depression than men, thought to be due in part to estrogens, which may alter the activity of neurotransmitters that contribute to depression.

Depression is not a recent phenomenon: in ancient Greece the condition was thought to be due to an imbalance in the four basic bodily fluids, or 'humours', and Hippocrates described the symptoms of 'melancholia' as all 'fears and despondencies, if they last a long time'. Buddha (Siddhartha Gautama 563–483 BC) is documented as suffering from depression in his early years, as are Samuel Johnson, Mozart, William Blake, John Keats, Abraham Lincoln and Winston Churchill, to name a few; the list is extensive.

The Church of the early Middle Ages was concerned very much with life in the hereafter rather than on earth, and this marked a general decline of interest in the healing arts. This was a period when belief in the supernatural was prevalent among the general population and although the Church did not deny its existence, it regarded any form of magic as evidence of communion with devils or in some cases with Saints. The best treatment offered usually involved the afflicted person being examined for any marks on the skin that the Devil may have left behind and placing holy relics on the offending area.

Houses in which the mentally ill were incarcerated and chained up in filthy conditions had been in existence since medieval times, but in the eighteenth and early nineteenth centuries hospital reformers set about improving the treatment of inmates, one of the most influential in regard to mental institutions being the Quaker Samuel Tuke. While living conditions were improved, an understanding of the causes and developing treatments for mental illness did not advance much during this time, and it was quite common for women experiencing post-natal depression to be confined to an asylum as their husbands and society could neither comprehend nor cope with the affliction. It was not until the twentieth century that methods of treatment – for example, electroconvulsive therapy (ECT) – rather than containment, started to become popular.

However, over the centuries, as these official doctrines regarding treatment of depression came and went, lay people continued to use the traditional herb and plant remedies that had been passed down through the generations to heal the sick, including for those suffering from black moods. These remedies included:

* taking cardamom seeds in some tea;

* eating apples with milk and honey every day;

* eating cashew nuts in order to increase the appetite;

* drinking lemon balm tea several times a day;

* eating half an onion a day.

# HEADACHES, MIGRAINES AND HANGOVERS

# Headaches

Most people experience the discomfort of a headache from time to time, which can commonly be brought on by stress, tension, eyestrain or dehydration. If you want to avoid the conventional method of reaching for the painkillers, here are a few traditional remedies:

❧ Drink six to eight glasses of water in quick succession to aid dehydration.

* Apply a poultice made from ripe banana peel to the painful area.

* Relieve stress and tension by drinking a cup of camomile tea several times a day.

* Place a slice of raw onion on the back of the neck.

# Migraines

It appears that mankind has always been afflicted with the curse of the migraine, a severe form of headache which, apart from a throbbing and debilitating pain, often has associated symptoms such as nausea, aversion to bright lights and noise and, for some sufferers, blurred vision and the appearance of bright flashing lights. The first descriptions of migraine headaches were recorded in the Mesopotamian era, around 3000 BC, and there have been an abundance of notable sufferers throughout history, including Julius Caesar, Napoleon, Vincent Van Gogh, Charles Darwin, Virginia Woolf and Sigmund Freud. The weird and colourful scenes described by Lewis Carroll in *Alice in Wonderland* and *Through the Looking-Glass* are attributed by some to have been influenced by his experience of recurring migraine episodes.

Early physicians attempted to treat migraines by inflicting yet more pain on the unfortunate sufferer by:

- ✤ drilling a hole in the skull to free 'evil spirits';

- ✤ applying a hot iron to the area of pain;

- ✤ making an incision in the temple and inserting a clove of garlic;

- ✤ purging;

- ✤ and, of course, the cure-all method of blood-letting.

We now know that migraines are caused by an imbalance of chemicals in the brain, which results in blood vessels becoming dilated and inflamed, and can be brought on by stress, tiredness, dehydration, skipped meals, or a reaction to certain food and drinks, the commonest being: cheese, chocolate, alcohol and drinks containing caffeine.

There are many drugs specifically prescribed to combat migraines, but here are some old-fashioned remedies:

❖ Ripe banana peel applied as a poultice to the sore area.

❖ A slice of raw onion placed at the back of the neck.

❖ Sniffing freshly grated horseradish. Also, application of a muslin cloth containing a mixture of grated horseradish and water to the painful area.

# Hangovers

The consumption of alcohol has traditionally been associated with the rituals and festivals of almost all ancient civilizations, some of which went on for days, and with them came the inevitable hangover.

In ancient Greece, the standard cure was to breakfast on sheep lungs and owl eggs, while the Romans favoured deep-fried canary and boiled cabbage leaves. The Vikings ate Lutefisk, dried cod that had been steeped in lye (a strongly alkaline solution). Its jelly-like consistency of animal fat and fish oil was thought to soak up any remaining alcohol left in the stomach. Later, the folk of medieval England swore by consuming a paste made from ground eels and bitter almonds.

Saint Bibian (or Vivian) is the patron saint of hangovers and torture victims – anyone who has experienced the resulting consequences of consuming too much alcohol will probably appreciate the irony. Also, the human body has not yet caught up with 'girl power' – women fair worse with hangovers because men have a higher percentage of water in their bodies, which helps to dilute the alcohol they drink.

Although there are some things that can help to alleviate the symptoms of headache, dizziness, nausea, vomiting and a very dry mouth, brought about by the chemicals found in alcoholic drinks called congeners, the best way of avoiding a hangover is to drink less. If you must indulge, however, here are a few sensible tips:

❖ Drinking water between alcoholic drinks does help to lessen the effects the next day.

❖ Clear spirits such as vodka and gin have fewer congeners than darker tipples such as whisky and brandy, and therefore tend to produce less intense hangovers.

❖ Eat before you drink. Eating after you are drunk will not help.

❖ Have a 'hair of the dog' – although drinking when you have a hangover is not a cure, it just delays the inevitable.

❖ Coffee worsens dehydration; avoid it if you have a hangover and drink water instead.

Old-fashioned remedies included:

* Eating asparagus before or after a night of drinking to ease a headache and speed up detoxification.

* Taking a tablespoon of honey, or adding a few tablespoons to your water or tea. This is believed to help to stabilize your blood sugar levels.

* Soaking in a bath of mustard powder to speed up the detoxification process of a hangover.

* Rubbing a slice of lemon under your armpits; also adding fresh lemon juice and a little sugar to a glass of water to help ease nausea and vomiting.

* Taking ginger tea to relieve nausea: steep fresh slices of root ginger in hot water for about ten minutes and then drink.

* Eating bananas to help restore depleted sugar levels.

# Eighteenth-century Drinking Habits

During the eighteenth century there was an unprecedented rise in the popularity of gin drinking in England, especially in London, and by 1743 the population was estimated to be consuming 2.2 gallons (10 litres) of 'mother's ruin' per head, across all levels of society. This lasted for several decades and led to a huge increase in drunkenness and related violence, crime and ill health, only finally being somewhat curbed by the Gin Act of 1751, which required it to be sold on licensed premises. William Hogarth vividly depicts the misery resulting from this epidemic of inebriation in *Gin Lane* (1751), and below are two very contrasting remedies to aid what must have been a population suffering from one continuous hangover.

*Hangover cure for the wealthy:*
12 lb butter
1 lb sliced onions
1 bottle of champagne
Camembert cheese

Sauté the onions in butter, then decant into a soup tureen. Pour in the champagne, cover with a layer of well-scraped Camembert and breadcrumbs. Bake in the oven until crisp.

*Hangover cure for the poor:*
Drink a cup of warm milk containing soot. Warning: soot is a carcinogen and is likely to cause cancer.

# APHRODISIACS, FERTILITY AND LOVE POTIONS

# Aphrodisiacs

The libido can wane for a wide range of reasons, including excessive alcohol consumption, poor diet, anxiety, old age, or just plain boredom. Over the ages, many myths have grown up around what can improve the sex drive. Some do have an element of truth; many do not.

❖ Rhino horn. In the East, the belief that rhinoceros horn contains properties that increase libido and sexual vitality has always been strong. This still continues today to the extent that rhinos have been hunted to near extinction by man's search to attain increased sexual prowess, despite the fact that exactly what these mystical properties are remains a mystery.

❖ Onions. These vegetables contain an abundance of nutrients, including fibre, folic acid, potassium and vitamin C, which contribute to general good health, including benefits to the heart and the circulation generally. This is probably why historically they have been considered an aphrodisiac – ancient Egyptians, Greeks and Romans all believed that consuming onions led to increased sexual performance, and the French still traditionally serve onion soup to newly-weds the day after marriage. [Tip: chewing a sprig of parsley can easily alleviate the potentially off-putting smell of onion breath.]

❧ Oysters. Casanova reputedly started his day by consuming around fifty oysters in order to maintain his insatiable sexual appetite. There may be some truth regarding the effects of oysters on the libido as they do contain amino acids that trigger increased levels of sexual hormones, as well as zinc, which, if lacking, can affect a man's sperm count and therefore fertility. Combined with the perceived similarity between oysters and female genitalia, oysters continue to be one of the most traditionally popular aphrodisiacs.

# Fertility

Stress often contributes to difficulties in conceiving. Old-fashioned ways of alleviating anxiety include:

❖ Camomile or lemon balm. Several cups of camomile or lemon balm tea per day help to relieve stress and tension.

❖ Lavender. Place a few drops of lavender essential oil on your pillow, or add to a warm bath and have a long soak.

In order to improve fertility (male and female):

❖ Increase your intake of essential fats – Omega 3 and Omega 6 – that are found in oily fish such as salmon, sardines, herrings and mackerel.

❖ Cut down on the amount of saturated fats you consume – these are found in meat and dairy products.

❖ Take a sensible amount of exercise – your fertility decreases if you are over- (or under-) weight.

❖ Try to buy organic food, as it is richer in nutrients free from harmful pesticides.

❖ Increase your intake of food that is rich in zinc: mangoes, pumpkin seeds and fish (oysters are particularly high in zinc).

# Love Potions

Throughout history, it seems that people have sought to influence the course of true love by means of various potions. Chaucer makes reference, in 'The Wife of Bath's Tale', to a wife administering a potion to stop her husband's wandering eye – the concoction certainly worked, it killed him!

Here is a love potion that should not do your prospective lover too much harm, if you can actually get him/her to drink it:

❧ Grind one handful of lovage blossoms, leaves, stems and roots into a powder.

❧ For one cup of tea, pour boiling water over one tablespoon of the powder, and let it steep for fifteen minutes. This should be sipped slowly.

If the tea does not tempt the object of your desire, then try this method of attracting him/her to you:

❧ Collect rainwater in a crystal glass or vase.

❖ Thinly slice an apple and place it in a saucepan with some rosemary, thyme, sea salt and cinnamon.

❖ Pour over the rainwater and simmer over a low heat for ninety minutes.

❖ Strain the potion into a jar.

❖ Dab the potion onto your pulse points every day for a week.

Apparently, your future lover will then become irresistibly attracted to you.

# The Celestial Bed

In the late eighteenth century, Edinburgh doctor James Graham invited wealthy childless couples to pay £50 (around £7,500 in today's money) for the privilege of spending a night in his 'Celestial Bed', which he claimed would radically increase their chances of producing offspring.

The huge bed, at his house in Pall Mall, London, was surrounded by magnetic fields and mirrors, with stimulating fragrances, a tilting frame which put couples in the best position to conceive, and musical accompaniments whose intensity increased in time with the ardour of the bed's occupants.

The bizarre methods of this pioneering sexologist eventually fell from favour with fashionable society as he was ridiculed by satirists and labelled a quack. He returned, bankrupt, to Edinburgh in 1783.

# MORNING SICKNESS AND MENSTRUAL PAIN

## Morning Sickness

Morning sickness in pregnancy usually subsides around the fourteenth week, although some mothers do suffer with the condition for the full term. Sickness is not necessarily restricted to the mornings, and can be triggered at any time of day by an aversion to certain smells or tastes. The sense of smell becomes more pronounced during pregnancy and odours that previously did not trouble an expectant mother become offensive, inducing vomiting.

It is best to stick to bland foods, eating little and often throughout the day. The symptoms can be relieved by using traditional methods such as:

❖ eating sliced bananas very slowly;

❖ adding about one teaspoon of apple cider vinegar to every 200 ml (8 fl. oz) of water, and sipping throughout the day and night;

❖ drinking ginger tea two or three times a day. To make the tea, place half a teaspoon of powdered ginger spice into a cup and fill with boiling water. Cover and let it stand for ten minutes. Strain and sip. The tea can be sweetened with a little honey if preferred;

❖ placing a slice of raw onion under each armpit;

❖ keeping a handkerchief scented with freshly squeezed lemon;

❖ sipping mint tea. Mint can minimize nausea by reducing the stomach's gag reflex. Make mint tea by placing one tablespoon of mint leaves in a pint jar of boiling water and let it stand for thirty minutes, shaking occasionally. Strain and sip.

# Menstrual Pain

Most women experience the discomfort of period pain, which can be particularly debilitating at the onset of puberty and during the teenage years. Conversely, older women who are approaching menopause may also endure very painful periods, but this is likely to be caused by problems related to the womb such as fibroids.

Menstrual pain manifests itself as a feeling of cramp in the lower abdomen, a sharp or aching pain that comes and goes, and possibly back pain, which is usually worse at the onset of a period.

During the Middle Ages, religion played a major part in all aspects of life, including medicine. The general consensus among doctors at the time was that menstruation was a sickness bestowed upon women by God as a punishment for Eve's original sin in the Garden of Eden and, as they deserved to suffer, no pain relief should be administered. As if to back up this theory, nuns who ate a strictly monastic diet lacked proper nourishment and often their periods would stop, which was seen as a sign from God of their holiness.

Women therefore had to rely on traditional remedies passed down from mother to daughter to try to alleviate menstrual pain. Below are some examples of old-fashioned methods of pain relief:

✤ Crush one to two tablespoons of fresh ginger and soak in a cup of hot water for ten minutes. Drink several cups per day. A teaspoon of honey can be added.

✤ Eat half an onion for several days preceding the onset of your period. Raw onion is more effective than cooked.

✤ Drink several cups of raspberry tea during your period.

✤ Exercising regularly tends to avoid more painful periods.

# Was Cannabis the Answer to Queen Victoria's Menstrual Pain?

During the nineteenth century, cannabis became a popular treatment for many ailments, including muscle spasms, menstrual cramps, and to promote uterine contractions in childbirth. Queen Victoria's personal physician, Sir Robert Russell, was a great believer in its use and wrote many papers extolling the benefits of cannabis, describing it as 'one of the most valuable medicines we possess'. He recommended it for easing menstrual pain and hence it is quite likely that the Queen would have been prescribed cannabis for this reason – she would not have smoked it; instead it would have been administered in the form of an extract in alcohol (tincture).

# INDIGESTION AND HEARTBURN

*'I have never developed indigestion from eating my words.'*

*Winston Churchill*

Indigestion, also known as dyspepsia, is a general term for feelings of pain and discomfort in the stomach and under your ribs, usually after eating, although indigestion can strike at any time and there are many different causes, from rich food and fizzy drinks to stress and eating on the go. Hippocrates, the father of modern medicine, believed, incorrectly, that atmospheric conditions had an effect upon human digestion and that strong winds blowing from the north were the principal cause of his dyspepsia. Henry

VIII's notoriously volatile temperament is thought to have been on account of him suffering with appalling indigestion. Henry's habit of gorging himself at banquets most likely made him a martyr to the tummy grumbles and yet his unwillingness to alter his eating habits led him to concoct bizarre remedies. One old wives' tale dating from the Tudor period states that listening to music while eating causes dyspepsia, and this led to Henry VIII banning all his court musicians from performing before or during banquets.

Some people get indigestion a couple of times a year, but others suffer every day with symptoms ranging from mild discomfort that lasts just a few minutes to severe pain, occasionally accompanied by nausea and vomiting, that goes on for several hours.

# Indigestion: Causes and Symptoms

The most common causes:

* Eating too much or too quickly, or eating at irregular intervals.

* Guzzling down sweet and sticky carbonated drinks.

* Excessive consumption of alcohol prior to or during meals.

* Eating and drinking acidic citrus foods and drinks, and spicy food.

* Eating while standing up or moving around.

* Medical complaints such as obesity, stress or depression.

The most common symptoms:

✤ Pain behind the ribs and a rumbling and gurgling stomach.

✤ A knotted stomach and feeling bloated and uncomfortable after eating.

✤ Suffering from stomach cramps and excessive burping and flatulence.

✤ Feeling sick and suffering from trapped wind.

Different foodstuffs trigger indigestion in different people and being mindful of this and the common causes can help to manage the problem effectively. There are several quick and easy old wives' remedies at hand, which can be cobbled together from ingredients in most kitchen cupboards.

Ginger has long been known to aid digestion and relieve dyspepsia. Ayurveda, a 5,000-year-old form of natural medicine from sub-continental India, makes liberal use of ginger, either brewed in tea or chewed before or after a meal to quell or deter stomach pains. Similarly, camomile tea has a soothing effect on the digestive system after a rich or heavy meal, as camomile contains an active ingredient that calms inflammation in the intestinal tract. Chewing and swallowing a spoonful of fennel or caraway seeds is another effective method of combating indigestion, as the seeds release natural oils that help quell stomach spasms and control flatulence. Alternatively, fennel seeds can also be used to make a tasty herbal tea that performs the same function but may be more palatable:

❖ Take three teaspoons of fennel seeds and a star anise and crush them into a fine powder with a pestle and mortar.

❧ Place the powdered seeds into a cup and pour on hot (but not boiling) water, stir and allow to cool before drinking.

Heartburn is an unpleasant condition related to indigestion that occurs when acid from the stomach rises up into the oesophagus and the throat, where it causes a burning pain, known in medical terms as acid reflux. Heartburn is becoming an increasingly common ailment thought to affect roughly one in three adults over the age of thirty. It is particularly prevalent in women during the latter stages of pregnancy. The pain can last for several hours or more and is often made worse by eating. Heartburn can also exacerbate insomnia, causing sleepless nights, because lying down can set off the condition.

The classic old wives' cure for heartburn is to ingest two to three tablespoons of cider vinegar with a little cold water either before or immediately after a meal. It may seem strange to be putting more acid into the stomach to quell an excess, but the cider vinegar helps to slow down the production of hydrochloric acid and neutralizes the acid reflex that prolongs heartburn.

# Kitchen Cures for Flatulence

*The fart is a fine old friend to man,*
*It gives the body ease.*
*It warms up the blankets*
*And chloroforms the fleas.*

Freedom from wind can be yours with these tried-and-tested remedies using store cupboard ingredients:

❖ Drink a mixture of warm water, ½ teaspoon of dry ginger powder, a pinch of asafoetida and a pinch of rock salt.

❖ Mix 2 teaspoons of brandy with a cup of warm water and drink before bed.

❖ Using a pestle and mortar, grind 1 teaspoon of pepper, 1 teaspoon of dry ginger and 1 teaspoon of green cardamom seeds. Add ½ teaspoon of this mixture to water and drink one hour after eating.

# COLD SORES AND MOUTH ULCERS

## Cold Sores

The name 'cold sore' implies that this virus only appears when someone is suffering from a cold, but this is not true. Cold sores are caused by the herpes simplex virus. You only catch this virus once, and when contracted you always have it, even though it may lay dormant for years. Some people are more prone to an outbreak of the virus than others, but roughly six out of ten people carry it.

You can initially catch cold sores by being kissed by someone who carries the cold sore virus, possibly when you are a child, and cold sores can be caught on any part of the body, although lips and genitals (genital herpes through oral sex) are the most common places. It is a myth that herpes simplex can be contracted through sharing cups, cutlery, towels etc., as direct contact with the skin is necessary. Herpes on the face is more likely to recur than genital herpes.

Herpes is the ancient Greek word for 'creeping', apt since the sores often spread across the skin. Due to an outbreak of epidemic proportions in Rome, Tiberius, Emperor from AD 14 to 37, outlawed kissing in order to curb the spread of the disease. Aulus Cornelius Celsus, who wrote extensively on medical matters around this time, was recommending that herpes should be treated by cauterizing the sore with a red-hot iron, so one would assume that the populous were reasonably happy to comply with the edict of Tiberius. Shakespeare makes reference to cold sores in *Romeo and Juliet*, describing blisters 'o'er ladies' lips', and in the eighteenth century the French government categorized herpes as a vocational disease of prostitutes.

The onset of a cold sore is usually signalled by an itch or tingling, although about half the time your immune system overcomes such symptoms before they develop fully. The first visible sign is a small red patch, followed by a blister or cluster of blisters. When the blisters burst they leave a small raw area that often takes a while to heal, since moving your mouth causes the scab to crack.

Common reasons for repeated outbreaks of the virus are tiredness, illness, stress, menstruation, too much alcohol or the ultraviolet rays from sunlight or sun beds. So, if you can determine what triggers your cold sores then you can try to take steps to prevent them.

There are numerous cold sore ointments available on the market but, if you want to avoid using chemicals on your skin, here are some old-fashioned remedies:

❖ Organic honey applied once the sore has opened up aids the healing process.

❖ Ice or cold herbal teabags such as mint, ginger or lemon balm should be applied before the sore has developed. Warm teabags can be applied to lesions.

❖ A fresh clove of garlic rubbed on the sore.

❖ Witch hazel applied daily to the sore.

# Mouth Ulcers

Mouth ulcers (also known as canker sores) can occur on the inside of the cheeks, the roof of the mouth, on the gums or on the tongue. These ulcers are small, circular white or yellow patches with a red, swollen ring around the outside and can be quite painful. They may appear as a single sore or in clusters.

The ulcers usually heal within seven to ten days and the most common causes include vitamin deficiency, certain food allergies, stress, poor dental hygiene, eating acidic foods, hormonal imbalance, bowel disease and skin disease.

Here are a few home remedies to treat mouth ulcers:

❖ Mix a teaspoon of salt and a few drops of water to form a thick paste. Carefully dry the area of the sore with a clean paper towel and apply the paste directly to the sore. It should be thick enough that the solution stays on your sore. Leave it until it has completely dissolved, then rinse your mouth out with water. Repeat twice a day.

❖ Place one teaspoon of baking soda into a glass, add a few drops of water and mix thoroughly to form a thick paste. Dry the sore with a paper towel, and apply the baking soda mixture directly. Leave the mixture on the sore until it dissolves completely. Repeat twice. Do this three times a day.

❖ Boil one teaspoon of coriander seeds in one cup (approx. 8 oz) of water. Allow to cool until warm and gargle. Repeat three to four times a day.

# CORNS AND FOOT FUNGUS

## Corns

Over the past few years, newspapers and magazines seem to have taken great delight in publishing photographs of the ugly and misshapen feet belonging to female celebrities, which have been brought about by wearing ill-supporting and often tortuous-looking footwear in the name of glamour.

Corns and calluses are caused by friction and pressure from skin rubbing against bony areas when wearing shoes, and are nature's way of protecting sensitive areas. Ignoring the first signs can lead to years of discomfort, and it is therefore wise to look after your feet by using a pumice stone to remove any deposits of hard skin every time you take a bath or shower. Moisturizing your feet after bathing (olive oil works well) also lessens the chances of developing corns, as does wearing shoes that fit properly and provide support.

If you do develop corns, they can be treated by using one of the following old-fashioned methods, which can be rather messy but do work:

* Secure a slice of lemon over the corn using tape and leave it overnight. Repeat this process until the corn has disappeared.

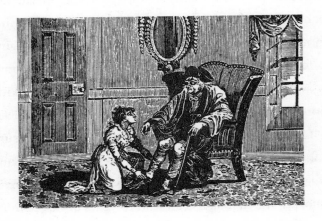

* Tape a moist tea bag to the corn or callus and leave for an hour.

* Keep feet soft by soaking them in a bowl of warm water and vinegar for half an hour.

* Exfoliate feet by adding a cup (8 oz) of oatmeal to a litre (35 fl oz) of boiling water and let it simmer until it has reduced down to about a quarter of a litre. Strain the mixture, let the water cool down until it is bearable and then soak the feet. Massage the oatmeal into the feet while soaking.

# Athlete's Foot

Athlete's foot is a highly infectious foot fungus that is usually picked up from swimming baths or other places where people walk barefoot (e.g. gyms, health clubs and spas). It starts between the toes and is extremely itchy; if left untreated it can crack and bleed, and in some cases go on to infect the nail.

Whether or not you have Athlete's foot, it is not advisable to go barefoot in communal changing rooms, but to wear slippers or shower shoes.

If you are suffering from this infection, ensure that you dry properly between your toes after bathing or showering. It is also advisable to wear white cotton socks, as these are best at combating sweaty feet; socks ought to be changed at least twice a day, if possible. You should also try to wear either canvas or leather footwear, as both plastic and rubber encourage sweating.

There are a number of natural remedies that will kill off the infection, one being to urinate on your feet when in the shower, which many people swear by. If you do not fancy trying this, here are some more tasteful methods:

❖ Make a massage oil from lavender, which contains antifungal properties, by adding three drops of lavender oil to one teaspoon of vegetable or olive oil, and rub into the infected area daily.

❖ Crush a clove of garlic and rub against the affected skin.

✤ Natural yoghurt is a quick remedy: either dab the yoghurt on to the affected area, and rinse when it is dry; or, if you have enough yoghurt, soak your feet in a bowlful.

✤ Combine white vinegar and salt and rub the mixture into your feet for three or four minutes. Dry your feet with a towel or hairdryer. Repeat twice a day and the infection should be gone by the third day.

# HAEMORRHOIDS

It appears that our ancestors have always suffered the curse of haemorrhoids (piles). Hippocrates (*c.* 460–375 BC) wrote horrific descriptions of the barbaric methods inflicted on patients in a bid to cure them. Their prevalence is also evidenced by the fact that during the Middle Ages, St Fiacre, as well as being the patron saint of gardeners, was also bestowed with the title 'Patron Saint of Haemorrhoid Sufferers'.

Today approximately fifty per cent of the population will experience the discomfort of this condition at some point in their lifetime. However, there appears to be fewer haemorrhoids sufferers in the Middle East and Asia, where the more natural position of crouching to evacuate is very common. In order to imitate this way of defecating in a way acceptable to Western sensitivities, toilet stools have been designed that heighten the position of the feet, allowing the body to function in the way nature intended.

Haemorrhoids are enlarged, painful veins around the anus or lower rectum that arise from increased pressure on internal or external veins around the anal canal. Internal haemorrhoids, unless they are severe, cannot be seen or felt, while external piles are visible around the outside of the anus. Although it can cause varying degrees of discomfort and embarrassment, the condition is not normally serious – this said, in acute cases, surgical treatment may be deemed necessary. For less severe episodes, there are a variety of creams and suppositories on the market containing anaesthetics and steroids that temporarily help to decrease inflammation. Below are listed some natural remedies that will reduce the discomfort associated with haemorrhoids, although these should also be accompanied by some simple but effective changes to diet that will help to improve the condition:

❖ Drink plenty of water (at least a litre per day, and more if you can manage it) to soften stools.

❖ Increase your intake of fresh fruit and vegetables.

* Add fibre to your diet – the range of bran-based cereals available has improved dramatically in recent years.

* Fruit juices are good for the prevention of haemorrhoids, especially dark berry juices such as blackcurrant and redcurrant.

* Increase your intake of foods that contain iron, i.e. chicken liver, prunes, dried apricots, sunflower seeds, pistachios, cashews, almonds, sesame seeds, baked potatoes, broccoli, tuna, ginger, garlic and onion.

* Avoid fried food, red meat, spicy food and pickles.

Natural remedies:

* Apply witch hazel to the affected area three times a day until the symptoms of piles go away. Continue treatment for two or three days afterwards to ensure they stay away.

* Take a warm bath three times a day. Do not add anything to the water and sit in the tub

for fifteen minutes. This relaxes the sphincter muscle and helps soothe the pain associated with haemorrhoid protrusions.

❧ Petroleum Jelly or Zinc Oxide Paste work just as well as costly creams. After a bowel movement, clean the area with water and dry (do not use scented toilet paper, soap or body wash), then dab a small amount of Petroleum Jelly or Zinc Oxide on a cotton wool ball and gently apply to the affected area.

Finally, and most importantly, if you feel the call of nature do not ignore it – if you regularly delay bowel movements you are encouraging the onset of piles.

# Could Haemorrhoids Have Influenced the Outcome of the Battle of Waterloo?

It is well documented that Napoleon was a long-suffering martyr to haemorrhoids and that one of the remedies prescribed by his physician was the application of leeches to his noble posterior. However, there is an account that Napoleon had succumbed to a particularly nasty bout of piles during the Battle of Waterloo and that in the melee the aforesaid physician mislaid the medicinal leeches and instead had to administer laudanum to alleviate the pain. Unfortunately for Napoleon, he was mistakenly given an overdose, which led to a temporary impairment to his famous ability as a military tactician.

# HAYFEVER

While most people revel in a hot summer's day, spare a thought for sufferers of hayfever and pollen-related allergies. Pollen counts during spells of hot weather have been increasing year on year, with current predicted levels being the highest for half a century and expected to more than double again in the next fifty years. Scientists are also concerned about the effects of global warming on increased pollen counts and fear that pollen is becoming more potent as it battles against unpredictable weather patterns. All of this is bad news for people with allergies, as an increase in the potency and dispersion of pollen will have an impact on the efficacy of antihistamine treatments.

The old wives recommended apples – either fresh or steamed – and medical evidence does suggest that a substance called quercetin found in apples acts as a natural antihistamine. Drinking lots of camomile tea and inhaling the steam also helps to relieve congestion. If using camomile tea bags, remove them after infusing the water, leave to cool in the fridge, and use them to relieve itchy and sore eyes by pressing them gently over the eye sockets.

Another traditional method of combating hayfever is to drink at least three glasses of elderflower cordial a day as spring approaches. Elderflowers contain active compounds that are thought to be anti-catarrhal, and so help to head off runny noses and blocked sinuses as the pollen season approaches. The cordial is very easy to make and has the added advantage of being fragrant and refreshing as well as good for you.

# ELDERFLOWER CORDIAL

## *Ingredients:*

25 heads of elderflower, rinsed
2 kg (9 lb) of soft brown sugar
2 litres (3.5 pints) of water
2 lemons, sliced

## *Method:*

✤ In a saucepan heat up the water, sugar and lemons, stirring gently until all of the sugar has dissolved.

✤ Once the mixture has cooled, place the washed elderflower heads in a covered container, pour over the mixture and leave to brew for at least three days.

✤ Strain out the elderflower heads, decant the liquid into bottles and store in a cool, dry place away from direct sunlight.

✤ Dilute roughly one part of the cordial to three parts water.

Nettle tea is another old-fashioned remedy, as stinging nettles contain natural antihistamines that can reduce the inflammation produced by the body during an allergic reaction. The tea is believed to ease nasal congestion, watery eyes, chest congestion and many of the other symptoms related to hay fever. To make the tea, simply wash the nettle leaves thoroughly and drain. Chop them finely and place about two teacupsful into a large teapot and steep in just-boiled water. Leave to brew for fifteen minutes and then pour through a tea strainer. Nettle tea is also thought to be good for the liver.

Other common remedies include raw onions, which also contain high levels of quercetin, and honey produced by local beekeepers.

# CONSTIPATION AND DIARRHOEA

Constipation and diarrhoea are the bookends of the spectrum of common bowel complaints. We all suffer from them from time to time and yet it is strange how reticent people are to discuss any difficulties they may be having with their motions. A lack of fibre in the diet or not imbibing enough liquids on a daily basis are the usual causes of constipation, although women often suffer during pregnancy and it is also a symptom of irritable bowel syndrome. Having a daily intake of fruit and vegetables can usually help to loosen up the bowels and ought to form an integral part of any balanced diet. The old wives were particularly fond of steamed cabbage leaves as a remedy, and bananas have long been recognized as not only an important source of vitamins but also a useful natural laxative.

More immediate remedies when suffering from constipation include drinking a mixture of hot water and molasses. Simply dissolve two teaspoons of molasses into water from the kettle and drink. Other useful tea infusions for relief from constipation include mixing liquorice root powder with water, or drinking ginger or peppermint tea. A simple preventative method is to swallow two tablespoons of olive oil every morning before breakfast.

Diarrhoea is most commonly caused by stomach infections, food poisoning and other viruses, and, although unpleasant and uncomfortable, it is usually a short-lived ailment. The most important remedy is to avoid dehydration by taking on as much fluid as possible. If symptoms persist, however, medical advice should be sought – increasingly, diarrhoea is being diagnosed as an indicator of a variety of medical complaints, such as lactose intolerance and Crohn's disease, and as a by-product of stress and anxiety.

Simple old-fashioned remedies include taking on added fibre by eating a bowl of porridge oats or muesli, as this can help to firm up the stools. A classic old wives' cure involves grating a whole apple and leaving it on a plate on a windowsill or in direct sunlight. Wait for around half an hour until the apple has gone brown, put the grated apple into a cup with some chunks of banana and mash together with a fork before eating. A bowl full of natural yoghurt with some tasty fruit such as strawberries or blueberries can also provide relief from the throes of diarrhoea. The live bacteria in the yoghurt promotes the production of lactic acids in the intestines, which are vital for combating bacterial infections from food poisoning and other viruses. Interestingly, the effectiveness of live yoghurt is very much at odds with an age-old myth that dairy

products exacerbate diarrhoea, particularly in young children, and should be avoided until the ailment has subsided. Although, understandably, people suffering from lactose intolerance should avoid dairy products, continuing to eat regularly and following a normal diet is vital in helping the intestinal system to recover quickly.

# PART TWO

# Remedies for Home and Garden

# CLEANING
# THE OVEN

There can be few household chores as arduous and unpleasant as cleaning the oven. The prospect of getting down, deep and dirty with a cooker that is caked completely in half-inch-thick congealed fat, blackened sludge and swathes of grease is enough to induce night sweats during the small hours for even the most fastidious and house-proud. Indeed, the act registers high on online household management discussion boards as one of the jobs people loath the most. It is little surprise, then, that specialist cleaning companies, devoted to oven cleaning, have emerged – but they come at a price. There is, however, an old-fashioned alternative to either paying for someone to clean the oven or spending seemingly endless hours scrubbing and scraping, which entails surprisingly little elbow grease.

First take a large ovenproof casserole dish, fill three-quarters with water and place in the oven. Set the oven to a high heat and leave for forty-five minutes. The oven will rapidly fill with steam from the boiling water and this helps to loosen the dirt and grime. Most professional oven-cleaning services use an expensive steam-cleaning apparatus, which essentially does the same thing. While the oven is steaming, take a container and mix one part of baking powder (bicarbonate of soda) with five parts of soda crystals (sodium carbonate), for example 100g (3.5oz) of baking powder to 500g (17.5oz) of soda.

Switch off the oven and allow it to cool for a minute or two, leaving the water inside. Open the oven door and remove the dish of water (be careful of burns as the steam will billow out). Once the steam has escaped, cover the sides and floor of the oven with the mixture (you may need to wet the sides to get the mixture to stick) and leave overnight or for at least eight hours. After allowing the cleaning blend enough time to work its magic, simply wipe the mixture and grease away and rinse with warm, soapy water. Any particularly stubborn grease stains may require a bit of scrubbing but this should be minimal compared to using commercial kitchen cleaning products.

# Baking Powder and the Manhattan Project

Bicarbonate of soda is most widely used as a leavening agent in the production of bread and cakes, hence its common name of baking powder. However, this humble chemical compound is a staple substance of many old wives' remedies ranging from cures for mouth ulcers to discouraging garden pests (it has even been known to be taken as an energy supplement by professional athletes). Of all its myriad of uses, however, perhaps the most obscure is the role baking powder played in the development of nuclear weapons. Scientists working on the Manhattan Project – the US-backed development of the atomic bomb during World War II – discovered that depleted uranium dust from nuclear fall-out contaminated cotton clothing and could not be washed out with conventional laundry detergent. However, by soaking the contaminated clothing in a solution of bicarbonate of soda the uranium oxide broke down and could be rinsed away with soap and water.

# AIR FRESHENERS AND NATURAL PERFUMES

The market for modern air fresheners is terrifyingly large, particularly in the United States, where an estimated three quarters of American households use some sort of product, either aerosol or electric, to deodorize their dwellings, generating massive profits running into billions of dollars. Add to this the commercial profits generated by corporate air fresheners – most office buildings and other institutions use some sort of air-freshening system – and the sheer sums of money involved becomes equivalent to the GDP of a fair-to-middling South American republic. Well maybe not quite, but pretty mindboggling nonetheless.

It should come as no surprise, then, that environmental groups have repeatedly flagged up the possible effects on our health and well-being of spending virtually our every waking hour breathing in the fumes of different chemicals. A 2007 study of supermarket-brand air fresheners by environmental pressure group the National Resource Defense Council found that many commercial air fresheners contained *phthalates*, which are chemicals used mainly in the manufacturing of plastics but also used as fragrance retainers. The use of phthalates in the production of children's toys has been banned in several US states due to health scares concerning their effect on hormonal development in adolescents.

Add to this the refusal of the big multinational conglomerates to actually come clean (no pun intended) and list the chemical ingredients used in manufacturing their products, and the seemingly benign world of air freshening starts to smell quite bad.

It is not part of the remit of this book, however, to jump on a hobby horse or espouse environmental conspiracy theories but it should be noted that we don't really know what we are breathing in when we spray an air freshener around in our homes. Thankfully, there are some simple, natural solutions to freshening up the home that are relatively cheap and easy and don't involve adding to the burgeoning profits of huge, faceless multinational corporations run by shape-changing lizards from the planet Venus (I think I may have gone too far in my Internet research on this topic).

The most simple method is to grow beautiful-smelling aromatic plants like jasmine, honeysuckle and tuberoses indoors – not only do they give off natural scents but they look great too. Placing bunches of dried herbs such as lavender, sage and spearmint around the home also provides lovely natural aromas.

Investing in a range of essential oils opens up a wealth of different remedies. Essential oils are available from most health shops and aromatherapists and also from online retailers. Although they may seem expensive for what you get (they are usually sold in 10ml bottles) they are powerful fragrances that stretch a long way and are well worth the expense.

Here are some more simple natural remedies to freshen up the home:

❖ Place lavender or southernwood sachets into clothing and linen drawers. These can be easily made by sewing together squares of old cloth and help to deter moths and keep drawer contents smelling clean and fresh.

❖ Gently rub drops of your favourite essential oil directly onto the wood in dresser drawers. The oil absorbs into the wood and has a slow release effect, but be sparing as essential oils are very strong and you may not want the scent to be overpowering.

❖ Fill the inside of a pillow or cushion with fresh pine needles and place on chairs or sofas to freshen upholstery.

❖ Smear the rims of the pots of window plants with an essential oil. Heat from the sun will warm up the oil and gradually release the aromas. The same effect can be produced at night by rubbing a couple of drops of essential oil on to light bulbs before turning them on.

❖ If you are lucky enough to have an open fire, add dried rosemary bush branches and cinnamon sticks to your kindling when you light the fire to create lovely warming scents.

❖ On cold winter days make a simple spice blend of cloves, cinnamon sticks, dried orange and lemon peel and a few cups of apple cider vinegar and water and simmer gently on the stove.

# AIR FRESHENER SPRAY

This spray is powerful and should be used sparingly to avoid the scents becoming too strong. Isopropyl alcohol can be purchased from most high street electronics stores as a cleaning agent for disc drives and other electrical equipment.

## Ingredients:

60 ml (¼ cup) isopropyl alcohol
25 drops bergamot essential oil
8 drops clove essential oil
5 drops lemon essential oil
240 ml (1 cup) distilled water

## Method:

❖ In a spray bottle, combine the alcohol and the essential oils and shake well to disperse the oils.

❖ Add the distilled water and shake for a minute or two more to thoroughly blend all the ingredients.

❧ Leave for several days before using to allow the fragrance to mature and the scents to infuse the alcohol and water. A few short squirts are usually all that is needed to produce a nice warming, spicy scent. Do not spray directly on to open flames, as alcohol is flammable. Store away from direct sunlight.

# CLEANING AND STAIN REMOVAL RECIPES FOR CARPETS, UPHOLSTERY AND FABRICS

Evidence exists that carpet-making began as far back as 6000 BC, and continued throughout the Middle and Far East, with carpets being used for tent furnishings, pillows and storage and for sleeping on by Nomadic tribes.

However, it was not until Tudor times that carpet was manufactured in Britain. The first person to do so was Robert Rothe, the first mayor of Kilkenny who, in 1537, imported Turkish weavers to create a rug for his estate; soon Cardinal Wolsey began to regularly import Turkish rugs. Thereafter, carpet manufacturing began in earnest, to adorn the floors and walls of those who could afford such things.

Carpets became more affordable with the onset of mass production, and nowadays most homes contain some type of carpet or rug. Fitted carpets were originally designed in the 1960s with the aim of reducing noise and retaining heat in public buildings, shops and offices, but soon became popular in family homes.

Upholstered furniture is a relatively new concept, which started to become fashionable in Europe around the beginning of the seventeenth century; materials such as sawdust, grass, feathers or animal hair were used to provide the padding on chair seats.

Of course, carpets and upholstery needed to be cleaned if the ornate and fashionable patterns and colours were to be fully appreciated, and various cleaning recipes were developed over the years.

# Carpet Cleaning

For best results, always sweep the carpet to make the fibres stand up and then vacuum thoroughly before cleansing.

## DRY SHAMPOO

### Ingredients:

½ cup cornstarch
2 cups baking soda
4 or 5 crumbled bay leaves
1 tbsp ground cloves

### Method:

❖ Thoroughly mix the ingredients, then sprinkle the mixture on to your carpet.

❖ Leave for an hour and then vacuum.

# SOLUTION FOR A STEAM CLEANER

## *Ingredients:*

vinegar

water

## *Method:*

❧ Mix 1 cup of vinegar with 10 cups of water.

❧ Add the solution to the steam cleaner. You should find it will clean the carpet and the cleaner at the same time, and that the smell of vinegar goes when the carpet is dry.

# The Most Expensive Carpet in the World

In 2009, the Pearl Carpet of Baroda sold for $5.5 million. In 1865, the 5´8˝×8´8˝ carpet was commissioned by the Maharajah of Baroda and was thought to be a gift for the tomb of the Prophet Muhammed at Medina. The surface of the carpet is covered with an estimated two million natural seed pearls and encrusted and embellished with hundreds of gold set diamonds and precious stones. Warning: Probably not wise to clean with vinegar or baking soda!

# Cleaning Upholstery

One simple method for cleaning upholstery requires nothing but neat white vinegar and a clean cloth. Soak the cloth in the vinegar and thoroughly wring it out, then gently wipe over fabrics to remove any surface dirt. The smell of vinegar does linger for a short while but eventually the furniture is left smelling fresh. Another method (overleaf) takes a bit more elbow grease, but the results are worth it.

# CLEANING FOAM

## *Ingredients:*

6 tbsp soapflakes
2 tbsp borax
1 pint (0.5 l) boiling water

## *Method:*

❖ Combine the ingredients until the mixture cools to a gel-like consistency .

❖ Using a whisk or a fork, beat the gel to a foam.

❖ Apply the foam to the fabric with a cloth or upholstery brush – do not soak the fabric.

❖ Wipe with a damp cloth.

# LOVELY LEMONY
# FURNITURE POLISH

This home-made furniture polish protects the wood surface, is durable and buffs up to a beautiful shine. Make a fresh batch before each polishing session.

## Ingredients:

olive oil

1 tsp lemon essential oil

## Method:

❖ Pour olive oil into a small cup and stir in the lemon essential oil.

❖ Mix the oils together thoroughly and apply a little at a time on to the wood with a soft cloth.

❖ Wipe dry with a clean, soft cloth, and buff up to a shining finish.

# Stain Removal

If you would rather not rely on chemicals, the remedy for removing stains from carpets, upholstery and fabrics can be found in most kitchen cupboards. Below are some solutions that require ingredients that are usually at hand. The key to stain removal is to act quickly to allow less time for the stain to set into the fibres and also to ensure that the mixture being applied is cool, as heat encourages the stain to set. Do not rub the stain because it will sink deeper into the fabric.

With carpets, if a spillage has just occurred then it is really important to remove as much of the liquid as possible with a paper towel. Fold and press layers of paper towel over the stains to absorb the moisture. Do this until all moisture has been absorbed. In order to remove tough stains such as urine, grass, coffee, wine or ketchup from carpets, you can use vinegar mixed with an equal amount of water. Simply spray or sponge on to the stain and leave for ten minutes before blotting with a paper towel. Another method is to sprinkle baking soda over fresh stains, allowing it to dry before vacuuming.

Below are various ways to remove stains on other fabrics:

## Stains on upholstery

✤ Apply a mixture of soda water and cornflour with a cloth, blotting the affected area. Wipe with a clean, damp cloth.

✤ Gently apply diluted white vinegar to the stain – do not rub, but leave for 10 minutes. Sponge off with clean water.

## Stains on clothing

✤ To remove stubborn stains such as blood, chocolate or coffee, make up a solution of 60 g (¼ cup) borax and 475 ml (2 cups) cold water. Soak the stain overnight and wash as usual.

✤ For tough coffee stains, beat an egg yolk into some cold water and spread over the stain. Rinse with cold water and repeat as necessary.

# Grease stains

❖ Make a paste of cornflour and water and apply to the stain. Leave to dry and then brush off.

❖ Sprinkle chalk dust or cornflour on to a fresh stain, then soak the fabric in a mixture of baking soda and water.

❖ For tougher stains, dab a little clear alcohol on the fabric before washing.

# Red wine stains

❖ Immediately sprinkle with salt then, when dry, brush away the salt and wash the fabric or clean the stain with soda water.

❖ Blot as much of the wine as possible with a paper towel. Soak the stained area in lemon juice, white vinegar, soda water, milk or white wine.

# Ink stains

* Wet fabric with cold water and apply a paste of cream of tartar and lemon juice. Leave for an hour before washing.

## Scorch marks

* Rub the affected area with half a raw onion and wait for the juice to be absorbed. Then soak in water for a few hours.

## Grass stains

* Brush off as much dirt, mud and grass as possible, then rub molasses or treacle into the stain. Leave for eight to ten hours before washing as usual.

# Mildew and Mould

Mildew can be tough to shift on fabrics and clothes and, furthermore, gives off an unpleasant and pungent aroma that standard washing often doesn't erase. The following remedy is an old family favourite that my grandmother showed me, and the solution usually works but may need a couple of washes. It is not advisable to use this method on dark-coloured or brightly patterned material, however, as too much lemon juice can cause bleaching marks to appear on the fabric.

# REMEDY FOR MILDEW

## Ingredients:

2 tbsp salt crystals
1 tbsp lemon juice

## Method:

❖ Take a small cup and add the salt crystals and lemon juice and mix together.

❖ Handwash the fabric in normal detergent but in warm rather than hot water, as too high temperatures can fix stains.

❖ Using a spoon, spread the solution over the mildewed areas and lay out to dry.

❖ After a couple of hours, rinse the fabric thoroughly in cold water. If the mildew persists repeat the process.

# UNBLOCKING DRAINS AND TOILETS

My grandmother always used to say to my younger brother, who harboured ambitions to learn a trade, that he should become a plumber, as then he would never be out of work. Not surprisingly, my ambitious sibling was less than enamoured with the thought of unblocking other people's drains and toilets for a living, and who can blame him (although I realize there is more to plumbing than just that). The chore of restoring a blocked toilet or drainage system to full functioning order is hardly one that anybody relishes, which is precisely why most people are prepared to pay the sizeable callout charge to have somebody come round and fix it for them. Add to this the fact that commercial cleaning products are expensive and damaging to the environment and it seems a no-brainer to get out the directory and call a plumber. There are, however, a couple of old wives'-style remedies that take little effort and often help to relieve the problem, if only temporarily. Both methods utilize those mystical and magical substances that have featured elsewhere in this book: namely borax, baking powder and vinegar.

To clean and sanitize your toilet bowl without using harmful bleach and chlorine products, and without getting too up close and personal with the toilet bowl for any length of time, simply prepare the following formula and leave overnight:

❖ First flush the toilet to wet the sides of the bowl.

❖ Take 250 g (approx. 1 cup) of borax and sprinkle around the inside so it sticks to the sides.

❖ Carefully drizzle 125 ml (½ cup) of vinegar over the borax, being careful not to wash the crystals off, and leave for several hours (preferably retire to bed).

❖ In the morning or several hours later, scrub off the mixture with a toilet brush and flush.

To unblock a kitchen or bathroom sink or small exterior drain you will need a box of baking powder and 475–700 ml (2 or 3 cups) of vinegar:

* Pour half a box of baking powder into the drain.

* Spoon the vinegar, a couple of tablespoons at a time, over the baking powder. The resulting effect is that the baking powder will foam up. Wait for a few moments for the foam to settle and repeat the process until all of the baking powder has dissolved. Leave for a couple of hours and do not use the drain during the resting period.

* Pour a kettle of boiling water into the drain to cleanse.

# Why Toilets are Called Thrones

It is widely believed that London plumber Thomas Crapper invented the common flushing toilet in the nineteenth century. This is actually not the case – not only was he not the inventor, but nor was he the first person to patent the invention. The honour of inventing the toilet actually goes to Elizabethan courtier Sir John Harrington (1561–1612). Harrington was something of a maverick character among the court and was reportedly referred to by Queen Elizabeth I as 'my saucy godson', on account of his ribald humour and risqué poetry (the childless monarch had over one hundred godchildren).

Harrington's best-known literary work is *A New Discourse of a Stale Subject, called the Metamorphosis of Ajax* (1596), a quasi-essay that purports to explain the workings of his new sanitary invention but was ostensibly a veiled political allegory about corruption and an excuse to libel prominent people Harrington disliked. The Ajax of the title was the name he gave to his flushing toilet – a play on the slang term for existing toilets, 'jakes' (largely just holes above shoots running down the sides of buildings and into the gutters of the streets below). Harrington's Ajax was installed in his ancestral home in the village of Kelston, Somerset, and the Queen is alleged to have tested it out when visiting Harrington, thereby becoming the first queen to sit on 'a throne', so to speak.

# OLD WIVES' WHOLESOME (AND NOT SO WHOLESOME) RECIPES

Meals eaten by many of our forebears would not sound particularly appetizing to us, with our modern palates and access to unlimited ingredients, especially those consumed by the poor. For the majority of our ancestors, their diet consisted of what was cheap and readily available.

# Middle Ages Meals

In medieval times, the diet of a peasant varied according to the season, as a large proportion of their calorie intake consisted of carbohydrates (various grains), and a poor harvest could have a big effect on their nutrition. The grains were either ground into flour to make bread, boiled whole in a soup or stew, or used to brew ale, with seasonal fruit providing some additional nutrients. Their protein intake came from beans, peas or lentils and sometimes fish; meat was a rarity and was too expensive for the table of a serf or peasant except on special occasions. Eggs, butter and cheese were often substituted for meat by the more prosperous.

Beer was drunk by both young and old in the Middle Ages because water was often contaminated and the brewing process helped to kill germs. Consuming three or four pints of ale a day was quite normal, and although some brews were strong, most ale was quite weak and was even taken at breakfast time.

Our lives are sedate compared to the majority of our forebears, who worked on the land and required far more food than us in order to function effectively.

The average modern man requires only 2,500 calories to maintain their weight (2,000 for a woman), whereas a peasant labouring in the fields for up to twelve hours a day had to take in between 3,500 and 4,000 calories to stay in reasonable health.

A staple part of peasant meals were soups, stews and pottage, containing ingredients such as peas, beans, cabbage, nuts, berries, leeks, turnips, carrots, parsnips, onions, parsley and garlic. However, nobles considered that vegetables that came from the ground were only fit to be eaten by the poor, which limited the sources of fibre and vitamin C consumed by the rich. Likewise, dairy products were also deemed to be inferior fare, and this led, ironically, to peasants generally being far healthier than their rich masters, who suffered from skin diseases, scurvy, rickets and bad teeth due to a diet that consisted mainly of meat (often dried, salted or cured), game (pheasants, deer, boar), fish, fowl and fruit, all of which were highly spiced.

During the Middle Ages, returning Crusaders had discovered new flavours on their travels and introduced the use of such spices as cinnamon, cloves, nutmeg, ginger, saffron, cardamom, coriander, cumin, garlic, turmeric, mace and star anise into European cooking. Sugar, which was first used as a sweetener by the Persians, also became popular with the rich around this time. Banquets were lavish, usually consisting of between three to six courses, with a great deal of effort going into the preparation and presentation, with exotic, magnificent food arrangements adorning the table. For example, jelly was made from peacocks, swans or pheasants, and their plumage, beaks and feet (which were also eaten) used to decorate the centrepiece.

One dish that used boiled, cracked wheat as its base was frumenty, from the Latin word *frumentum*, meaning 'grain'. An Old English recipe for frumenty reads as such:

> *To make frumente. Tak clene whete & braye yt wel in a morter tyl the holes gon of; seethe it til it breste in water. Nym it up & lat it cole. Tak good broth & swete mylk of kyn or of almand & tempere it therwith. Nym yelkes of eyren rawe & saffroun & cast therto; salt it: lat it naught boyle after the etren ben cast therinne. Messe it forth. (Curye on Inglysch CI.IV.i.)*

This dish, or variations of it, has been made since the Middle Ages, and was typically served in winter as a symbol that spring would soon come, as well as traditionally eaten on the festival of Twelfth Night. The recipe overleaf is quick to make and an excellent accompaniment, especially with highly flavoured meat.

# SWEET FRUMENTY

## Ingredients (serves 6):

140 g (5 oz) cracked wheat
1 pint of ale or stock
½ tsp of cinnamon, nutmeg and ginger
1–2 handfuls of currants
2 beaten eggs
3–4 tbsp single cream
pinch of saffron

## Method:

❖ Mix the cracked wheat with the ale or stock and boil for fifteen minutes. Let it stand for a further fifteen minutes until most of the liquid is absorbed. The mixture can be topped up with a little more water or stock if it begins to dry out too much.

❖ Add the cinnamon, nutmeg and ginger and boil for a few minutes until the wheat is soft.

❧ Remove from the heat, add the currants and allow the mixture to cool a little.

❧ Stir in the beaten eggs and single cream and, if you wish, add a pinch of saffron.

❧ Cook through on a low heat – do not allow it to boil.

# Plague Cure

During the fourteenth century, the plague killed more than a third of Europe's population and people desperately sought to find remedies to ward off or cure this deadly disease. All manner of strange concoctions were created in an attempt to aid victims. Here is one such recipe:

❖ Crush a few leaves from the following plants: feverfew (for fever and head-aches), scabious (for the scabs and itching), mugwort (a general plague protector), wild briar (a laxative to purge the body), mallow (for aches and pains), yarrow (to heal wounds), and sage (to help ease joint pains).

❖ Stir in grape juice, wine, ale or, if preferred, the victim's own urine.

❖ Strain the mixture through a cloth and drink.

# The Victorian Poor

If peasants in the Middle Ages were relatively healthy, the same cannot be said for their Victorian descendants, who were very undernourished, with rickets and anaemia being endemic.

In towns and cities, most households relied on open-fire pan cooking as they had no ovens, and many had to contend with only one cooking pot in which to produce a hot meal, often comprising such ingredients as tripe, slink (prematurely born calves), or broxy (diseased sheep) if they were fortunate enough to acquire it, along with other rancid meat scraps they could get from the butcher.

For the unemployed, survival depended on whatever rotten vegetables and refuse scraps they could get their hands on, and therefore being placed in the workhouse, where at least they were provided with a diet of potatoes, cheese, bread and gruel, probably seemed preferable.

# How to Make Gruel

Gruel, which consists of cereal boiled in water or milk, is a thinner and less appealing version of porridge. In Victorian times, it formed an integral part of any workhouse menu. Here is how it was made:

❖ Mix 3 dsp of oatmeal with a little cold water to form a paste.

❖ Boil a pint (0.5 l) of water in a pan, add the mixture and boil for ten minutes.

❖ Add a couple of pinches of salt.

In the nineteenth century, with regional variations, the rural poor generally survived on wild birds, inexpensive meat (if they could afford it), bread, butter, potatoes and beer, the type and amount of food available depending on the season. One rural cookbook, *Esther Copley's Cottage Cookery* (1849), contains recipes for potato pie, stewed ox cheeks and mutton chitterlings, which sheds some light on to what some of those working on the land were consuming.

# Yorkshire Pudding

In some parts of the North of England, Yorkshire pudding is still traditionally eaten as a first course, this being a throwback to times when people needed 'filling up' as there was not enough meat to go round. Meat was usually spit-roasted and the pudding batter was placed underneath to allow the fat and juices to drip into it. Children were often given only batter pudding and gravy, while the meat was divided among the adults in the family.

# Wealthy Victorians

As a result of the Industrial Revolution in England, many peasants swapped their rural poverty for a life of toil in the factories, living in the overcrowded and rapidly expanding cities, where conditions were grim and food scarce. On the other side of the coin, the Industrial Revolution did create a new abundance of wealth for those who invested in the new mechanization and, by the beginning of Victoria's reign, a class of nouveau riche had evolved who were very keen to display their affluence at every opportunity.

Mealtimes provided an ideal platform from which to flaunt a family's prosperity, and became quite an event in the wealthy Victorian home. Even breakfast was an elaborate occasion in which eggs, bacon, ham and fish were served, alongside a variety of fruits. Lunch was usually a light affair, followed by afternoon tea, introduced by the Victorians, which gave the lady of the house an opportunity to show off her best silver, china and linen. Evening meals were usually served in four courses, with different wines to accompany each course, and Madeira and sherry at the conclusion of the dinner.

Oysters had become popular as an appetizer, and the second course was usually soup with a serving of fish. The main course was normally roasted meat or poultry with a variety of vegetables, freshly baked bread and sometimes pasta. Dessert would comprise several puddings and cakes, alongside a choice of cheeses and fresh fruit.

Given all the choices available at the affluent Victorian table there was a huge amount of waste, which seems shameful at a time when the majority of the population were living on the bare minimum or less. Leftover food was usually offered to the household servants and anything they did not consume was then passed on to the poor. However, without refrigeration one might wonder what condition the scraps were in by the time they reached the bellies of the impoverished recipients.

# Expansion of the Empire

As the Crusades had influenced the flavour of food in Britain during the Middle Ages, so too did the acquisition of the Colonies, with the British Empire extending to over one-fifth of the globe during Queen Victoria's reign. Everything Indian appeared to be popular at this time, which saw the introduction of curry powder and variations on Indian dishes, although these would probably have not been recognizable to an Indian. A popular breakfast dish was kedgeree, still eaten today but now usually at lunch or supper.

# KEDGEREE

## Ingredients:

3 hard-boiled eggs

700 g (25 oz) haddock fillets

1 pint (0.5 l) water

1 medium onion

100 g (3.5 oz) butter

2 tsp curry powder

220 g (8 oz) long-grain rice

3 tbsp parsley

juice of half a lemon

## Method:

✤ Roughly chop 3 hard-boiled eggs and set aside.

✤ Place the haddock fillets in a large pan, and cover with cold water. Bring to the boil, then reduce the heat, cover and leave to simmer for eight minutes.

❖ Remove the haddock from the pan and place in an ovenproof dish, cover with foil and keep warm in a very low oven.

❖ Pour the cooking water into a jug and set aside.

❖ Finely chop a medium onion. Melt the butter on a low heat, add the onion and fry for five minutes until soft.

❖ Add the curry powder, stir and cook for one minute.

❖ Stir in the long-grain rice and add 450 ml of the saved fish water. Stir well and then simmer for fifteen minutes.

❖ While the rice is cooking, remove skin from the haddock and flake into a dish.

❖ When the rice is cooked, add the fish, eggs, the roughly chopped parsley and the lemon juice. Gently stir together. Add salt and pepper to taste.

❖ Place the lid back on the pan and leave on a very low heat for another four minutes, then serve it in the warm ovenproof dish.

# Anyone for Hedgehog?

Hedgehogs are becoming a rarity and, sadly, many of us only get to see those that have been unfortunate enough to have unsuccessfully navigated a busy road. However, in the past these creatures were plentiful and, for our ancestors, a popular source of meat.

The most common method for cooking hedgehog was to cover them in clay, bake them in a fire, and when cooked remove the hardened clay along with the spines. It was also a common belief that eating hedgehogs would cure a range of ailments, including leprosy, colic, boils, gallstones and poor eyesight.

The following are ancient instructions for cooking hedgehog (source: Medivalcookery. com/oddities):

*Hedgehog should have its throat cut, be singed and gutted, then trussed like a pullet, then pressed in a towel until very dry; and then roast it and eat with cameline sauce, or in pastry with wild duck. Note that if the hedgehog refuses to unroll, put it in hot water, and then it will straighten itself.*

# PLANTING AND SOWING

An integral part of any gardening enterprise is methods of planting and sowing. It stands to reason that if you plant your seeds effectively you have a better chance of reaping the rewards. Plant seeds badly and more than likely nothing will grow, or if it does the outcomes may prove insubstantial and disappointing. It is therefore not surprising that gardeners' folklore has many variations on the theme of how best to plant seeds. The most well known is perhaps the old rhyme: 'Scatter your seeds in a row, one for the mouse, one for the crow, one to die, one to grow.' In short, this is old-fashioned home-spun common sense: not all seeds or seedlings will germinate and birds and other wildlife feed off plant seeds (field mice are thought to store seeds for the winter by digging them up), so the best option is to plant plenty in the knowledge that not all will survive.

Other old wives' lore centres on the best time of year to plant and sow. One particular tradition is the planting of potatoes on Good Friday. On the face of it this seems absurd, as the date of Good Friday can vary by up to five weeks from one year to the next. One possible origin for the tradition is that it dates back to rural Ireland, a country renowned for its love of potatoes. Strict Irish Protestants were forbidden to eat potatoes on the grounds that they are not mentioned in the Bible. As the potato crop became an important staple of the rural Irish peasantry, the religious question was neatly sidestepped by blessing the seeds and planting them on the holiest of days.

Alternatively, the tradition of planting on Good Friday could also be seen as an early example of biodynamic gardening. There has been increased interest in biodynamic gardening in recent years, the basis of which is determining when to plant seeds according to the cycles of the moon. The old wives' mantra of 'never sow seeds when the moon is waning' suggests that just after a full moon is the best time to plant. In scientific terms, the cycles of the moon affect the tides and water tables, making it possible that there

will be rainfall after a full or new moon, which will help newly planted seeds to germinate. As the date of Good Friday is determined by lunar tables, with Easter Sunday being the first Sunday following the first full moon after Passover (the Paschal Full Moon), it is possible that there was also an observable biodynamic, as well as religious, reason for choosing Good Friday as the ideal day to plant.

There is a wealth of advice concerning tips and tricks of the trade for planting and sowing different vegetables, flowers and fruits. One classic piece of lore concerns rotating the planting of herbs in different positions around the garden. This is thought to originate from the work of renaissance-era botanist John Gerarde (1549–1611), the author of *The Herball*, one of the first books published in English about gardening. Gerarde maintained that changing the positions of different herbs and switching, year on year, 'hot' herbs (such as thyme) that drink the soil dry of nutrients with 'cold' herbs (such as mint) that replenish the soil. Other less scientific and more superstitious tips include burying beef dripping under rose bushes (although beware of passing foxes decimating your rose garden to get at the dripping) and mixing mothballs into the topsoil just prior to planting rows of carrots.

# WARDING OFF INSECTS AND OTHER ANIMALS

In the natural order of things one would think that insects, by and large, have a symbiotic relationship with plants. Let nature take its course and see what happens. While there are many examples of symbiosis between species, the classic example being bees and flowers, sadly there are many garden pests that, in short, bring little to the table in terms of what scientists refer to as 'mutualism', and some can be quasi-apocalyptic in their appetite for destruction. Global warming has no doubt had a profound effect in this respect, as adverse and unpredictable weather patterns continue to unbalance whatever fragile equilibrium there may be between plants and insects. Although history, of course, can point to many examples of periods of drought and famine, and the Bible is full of floods and plagues of locusts etc. so to some extent there is no real solution to avoiding acts of God.

Most experienced gardeners have a fairly good grounding in which mini-beasts are benign and which are malign, but as a rule of thumb the old adage: 'If it moves slowly stamp on it; if it doesn't, leave it be' is useful – some insects have natural predators such as spiders that help to regulate the natural balance of a garden's insect population.

There are some common garden beasties such as slugs, caterpillars and aphids that can cause catastrophic damage to plants and crops of vegetables. Not all slugs and caterpillars are harmful, but for the hearty amateur it takes some research (or a degree in entomology) to distinguish one slug from another, as there are over thirty different species in the UK alone.

There are a variety of different pesticides and insecticides available at most garden centres, although the jury is very much out on their efficacy and the ecological side effects of swamping your garden in chemicals. The old wives, of course, had to rely upon their own ingenious methods and practices to combat garden pests with whatever they had close to hand. Overleaf are some common remedies that, although not always foolproof (the little critters are very persistent), can nonetheless provide some respite from ravaging insects.

# Slug Pubs

Slugs love beer, particularly stale brown ales and bitter. Take a small-ish empty aluminium food tin and half bury it in the beds of the crop you want to protect (such as cabbages or lettuces) with the lip of the tin protruding just above the surface. Pour in about a cupful of stale ale. The slugs are attracted by the smell of the beer and can't resist a quick drink in the 'slug pub' on their way to the vegetable plot. Unfortunately, the beer is toxic to them and they are prone to slither in, sup up and drown.

# Walking on Eggshells

Garden slugs, snails, cutworms, caterpillars and other types of crawling garden pests can also be kept away by spreading crushed eggshells, nut shells, or even spent coffee grounds on the surface of the soil surrounding plants. The added benefit is that all these items add nutrients to the soil and decompose naturally.

# Plant Collars

The tender young stems of growing seedlings (which slugs and caterpillars love to scoff), such as tomatoes and other vegetables, can be protected from pests by making a metal collar and placing it around the stem. The insides of toilet rolls covered in aluminium are useful for this but make sure the collar isn't impeding the stem and there is sufficient space for it to grow. Placing small offcuts of copper piping into pot plants or around vegetable beds can also deter snails.

# Planning your Planting

It has long been known to the old wives that successful garden management depends not only on when to plant and sow but also where to plant and sow. By carefully planning the layout of the different beds it is possible to deter insects from venturing to certain parts of the garden without recourse to the gardening equivalent of chemical warfare.

# Onions and Garlic

These can be planted freely throughout the garden and help keep pests away from cabbages, broccoli, tomatoes, strawberries, peppers, cucumbers and more. Intercropping a few with all of these plants can greatly reduce garden pests.

# Sunflowers and Marigolds

As well as adding colour and beauty, these plants are hardy and a great trap crop for aphids and other pests. Marigolds, although seen less commonly these days, were traditionally a mainstay on the borders of most country gardens as the bouquet the flowers omit is noxious to many insects and the sap excreted from their roots helps to kill eelworm, which is particularly harmful to potato crops.

# Averting Aphids

Aphids such as the dreaded greenfly and whitefly kill plants by sucking the sap out of them. Two simple deterrents without recourse to insecticides are finely chopped banana peel mixed into the topsoil around plants, and cloves of garlic pressed into the soil. Both help to deter aphids and have the added advantage of providing potassium and other nutrients for the soil. In addition, you can also try making your own natural insect sprays free from synthetic chemicals (see recipes overleaf).

# TOBACCO JUICE PLANT SPRAY

## Ingredients:

0.5 oz (12.5 g) pipe tobacco
3 litres (5 pints) warm water

## Equipment:

spray bottle
sieve

## Method:

❖ Soak the tobacco in the warm water and allow it to infuse for a couple of days, stirring the mixture at regular intervals.

❖ Strain the mixture using a fine sieve to remove the tobacco.

❖ Transfer the tobacco-infused water into a spray bottle and use on plant leaves and stems of flowers such as roses to kill and deter a wide range of plant-damaging insects. Use as required but avoid spraying edible fruit and vegetables.

# GARLIC AND HOT PEPPER
## SPRAY

Use once a week or more for several weeks before and during infestation times.

## *Ingredients:*

2–4 cloves garlic

4 hot chilli peppers (e.g. Scotch bonnet)

2 tbsp sunflower or olive oil

1 tbsp washing-up liquid

2–3 cups hot water

# Equipment:

blender
strainer or coffee filter
spray bottle
gloves

# Method:

❖ Place garlic, peppers, oil, soap and water in a blender and blend on high for several minutes (or use a hand-held blender). The soap will bubble up at first.

❖ Leave overnight in a bowl for the garlic and peppers to infuse.

❖ Strain and store in a glass jar.

❖ To use, pour about 2 tbsp in a 16 oz spray bottle (or 3 tbsp in a 24 oz) and shake well.

❖ Spray directly on plants as required but make sure you wear gloves when applying and keep away from contact with skin and eyes.

# COMPOSTS AND SOIL NUTRIENTS

'Behold this compost! behold it well!' wrote American poet Walt Whitman in his classic collection of elegies to nature and free spirit *Leaves of Grass*. Although the thought of having a large pile of often foul-smelling waste, steaming and bubbling in the hot sun on a beautiful summer's day, may not seem the best way to be enjoying the joys of nature, composting and treating soil nutrients is a type of alchemy practised and understood by old wives through the ages.

There are several great advantages to composting. It takes a minimal amount of work, is easy and inexpensive and is an ecologically sound way to not only strengthen your garden, but help conserve and re-use resources and keep everyday household waste out of the clutches of municipal waste disposal services and landfill sites. The term composting refers to the decomposition of organic material over time with the end result being dark, moist, earth-like matter that can be used as a fertilizer to enrich soil or as soil for pots in which to plant bulbs directly. Bags of industrially produced compost are available in most garden centres, as compost is essential for anybody taking their home-growing remotely seriously. But it really is so simple to start a compost heap and make your own super-charged organic matter.

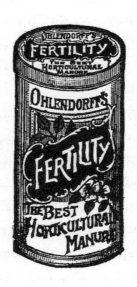

The starting point should be to save choice organic scraps from your kitchen. Great compost material such as banana skins, tea bags, egg shells and vegetable peelings are all perfect candidates for the process yet get tossed idly in the bin. When put together in either a specially made compost heap or a commercially bought compost bin and left over time, miniscule microbes feed on all this decomposing organic matter and, with the aid of bugs and worms, turn it into fertilizer and nutrient-rich plant feed. Those magical microbes, however, do require some tender loving care to help them to work their magic.

Like all living organisms, the little mites need feeding and there are two kinds of food that compost microbes require in order to break down organic matter. First is the organic matter itself (vegetable waste, etc.) and second is dead organic matter – anything from wilted flowers to grass cuttings, hay and sawdust – which provide valuable sugars or starch to add to the mix.

Cardboard also composts well and helps to soak up and retain moisture but be careful to use only plain cardboard as that which has been printed or coated in protective plastic does not decompose. It is also advisable to pour over used coffee granules and tea leaves and the water from peeled vegetables from time to time to add much needed moisture during hot spells. Finally, composts need some occasional exercise, so a regular turning with a pitchfork is advisable, while adding fresh peelings or dead grasses into the mix can often speed things up considerably. Behold the compost!

# WEEDING
# AND PLANT
# PROTECTION

Weeds, along with insect pests, are the curse of the gardener. The novice may at first find the practice of weeding to be valuable physical exercise, almost therapeutic, but this soon wears off as the task of controlling weeds that seem to spring up overnight quickly descends into a battle of epic proportions. Many organic-minded gardeners are opposed to the use of chemical weed killers as they can strip the soil of vital nutrients and are not especially ecologically sound. There are several non-chemical methods that can be used in the war on weeds, although, in truth, none of them will result in never having to spend time pulling the persistent nuisances out by the roots.

The most effective way to prevent weeds is to mulch. Mulch in a general sense is any substance or material that is spread or laid over the surface of soil in a two- to four-inch (5–10 cm) layer as a form of covering. Mulching works by depriving the seeds of sunlight and air needed to germinate and grow, while also keeping the undersoil cool and helping to retain moisture. Organic mulch improves soil fertility as it decomposes but needs to be regularly replaced as it breaks down. The best mulches are provided by the lovely rich compost from the home-made compost heap (see Composts and Soil Nutrients). Wood or shredded bark chips can also be used but are slower to decompose and do not replenish the soil with more vital nutrients. Straw or dry grass can also be effective and break down quickly. One top tip I received from an old wife was to collect sacks of pine needles: pine needles have a waxy coating that retains beads of rainwater and help to moisten the soil.

Old newspapers can also make great mulches, either by shredding the paper into strips and scattering on the beds (although on windy days they could blow all over the garden like a ticker tape parade) or by laying down a layer of newspaper at least four or five sheets thick and weighing it down with pebbles or small rocks. The same method using sheets of cardboard from collapsed cardboard boxes will also go a long way towards killing the weeds underneath. The weeds that are already there will die from lack of sunlight and their seeds will not be able to sprout. Cardboard is also useful to protect beds from the damaging effects of spring frosts, and can also be used as a shield to protect other plants when spraying.

Another method for killing weeds involves a kettle of boiling water. Boiling water is a great way to clear out vegetation on a wholesale basis and works especially well on pathways and paving stones. If used carefully it can also decimate weed patches but caution is required as boiling water is not selective. It will cook and instantly kill any plant that it comes into contact with, and this includes underground roots of nearby plants.

The old wives' staple of vinegar (either white or apple cider) diluted with water may be poured directly onto weeded areas, or dispensed more sparingly in a spray bottle. The acetic acid in the vinegar works to kill the leaves on the plant but does not affect the root. Vinegar is effective on any plant but works best on young plants because they do not have enough energy stored in the roots to regrow their leaves. If vinegar is applied to more established weeds enough times, the plant will eventually deplete its stored energy reserves and die.

Sprinkling rock salt judiciously on areas with weeds will also help to combat them but use sparingly as salt can devastate plant life and damage soil nutrients. In the Middle Ages, armies would often salt the fields of countries they were invading to destroy crops and demoralize and starve their opponents.

# HOME-MADE WEED KILLER

## Ingredients:

gin
tonic
apple cider
organic washing-up liquid

## Method:

❖ Mix a gin and tonic (1 part gin to 2 parts tonic) and leave for the tonic to go flat (so all of the carbonated gas escapes – well, most of it anyway).

❖ Pour the flat gin and tonic into a large jug and add a cup of apple cider vinegar and a squirt of organic washing-up liquid and stir.

❖ Add a cup of sterilized water, stir again and pour into a spray bottle.

❖ Spray the mixture directly on the leaves and roots of the weeds as required.

❖ Retire to a garden chair and sip a second gin and tonic (if you so wish) and let the weed killer do its business. The sprayed weeds will die and will be easy to pull out by the roots.

# PREDICTING THE WEATHER

Talking about the weather, or more precisely, complaining about the weather, is perhaps understandable given the vagaries of the climate these days, when a seemingly bright sunny day can cloud over rapidly, which accounts for the mainstay of modern meteorological speak, where terms such as 'changeable' and 'unsettled' prevail in weather forecasts. For our ancestors, however, predicting the weather was no idle or inscrutable pastime but quite often vital for survival and well-being. A wealth of old wives' folklore is concerned with predicting changes in the weather, often quaintly dressed up in little rhymes and poems that could be easily passed on to children and future generations. The old wives, as with much of their folklore, came to their conclusions through careful observation of nature and natural phenomenon. They may not have had the scientific evidence to back up their predictions, but modern understanding of meteorology has proved, at least in part, that there is actually some truth underpinning their beliefs. Collected below are a few of the old wives' weather-related rhymes and sayings with their origins.

# March Comes in Like a Lion and Goes out Like a Lamb

This refers to the likelihood of stormy weather at the beginning of March at the turning point between winter and spring. It expresses, more by hope than judgement, the probability of calmer weather at the end of the month. There are various printed origins for this phrase: it appears in a Jacobean-era drama *A Wife for a Month* by playwright John Fletcher, and in several farmers' almanacs in the early to mid seventeenth century.

# April Showers Bring May Flowers

Another piece of rather optimistic weather-related folklore that on the surface expresses the hope that rain in April upon the warming spring earth will help flowers to grow and bloom. The phrase was first used in print by sixteenth-century English poet Thomas Tusser, in his famous collection of proverbs *A Hundreth Good Pointes of Husbandrie* published in 1557. Tusser's book is a miscellany of tit-bits of advice and old wives' lore that range from the practical to the surreal (including an allegorical and faintly scandalous description of the attributes of good cheese). Tusser is also thought to be the author of the well-known phrase 'a fool and his money are soon parted'. The phrase 'April showers bring May flowers' also has a consolatory tone, suggesting that setbacks or misfortunes will be followed by more prosperous conditions.

# Cold is the Night When the Stars Shine Bright

This, like many old wives' weather predictions, is based on sound observation. Stars are more clearly visible at night when there is little or no cloud cover and although in warmer periods of the year heavy cloud often indicates rain, it also acts to insulate the earth and deter warm air from rising into the atmosphere.

# A Rainbow in the Eastern Sky, the Morrow Will Be Fine and Dry

# A Rainbow in the West That Gleams, Rain Tomorrow Falls in Streams

The weather systems in the northern hemisphere predominantly travel from west to east. Therefore, given that rainbows are caused by rain falling through sunlight, if the rainbow is in the east at the end of the day the rain has already passed by, whereas if the rainbow is in the opposite direction it is likely to be heading towards the observer. The proverb is of course reversed in the southern hemisphere where weather fronts travel in the opposite direction.

# If Birds Fly Low, then Rain We Shall Know; If Birds Fly High, Then Clear Blue Sky

Careful observation of the behaviour of animals underpins a lot of old wives' lore concerning the weather. The old adage that when cows sit down it is a sign of rain has recently been scrutinized in the United States by the University of Arizona. The scientists believe that cows lie down to conserve energy and their body heat, since their body temperature drops when they are standing up. As a change in the weather is usually preceded by a drop in temperature and the onset of low pressure, the theory is that the cows sit down to keep warm.

The saying 'If birds fly high . . .' also has a direct correlation with changes in air pressure. Birds, as a matter of practical necessity, fly lower during periods of low pressure as the air is thinner and harder to fly in. Conversely, in clear, cloudless days of high pressure they can fly higher and are easier to observe in the sky.

# How the Onge Tribesmen Cheated the Tsunami

On the 26 December 2004, a massive earthquake beneath the Indian Ocean caused a huge series of tsunamis to sweep across the sea devastating coastal communities in fourteen countries and claiming the lives of an estimated quarter of a million people. In the eye of the ensuing storms were the Andaman and Nicobar islands, a remote archipelago sparsely populated by tribes of hunter-gatherers. In the aftermath of the earthquake, it was assumed by rescue workers that the primitive tribesmen would almost certainly have been wiped out by the giant waves, as they were largely subsistence fishermen who lived in small coastal communities. To the surprise of Indian air force volunteers flying over the island, the majority of the Onge tribespeople of the Andaman Islands had survived. Further investigations confirmed that the tribes had suffered few if any casualties. Anthropologists believe that the key to the Onges' survival stemmed from traditions and knowledge relating to their folklore, based upon thousands of years of oral history passed down from generation to generation. Acute observation of minute changes in patterns of waves and the flight of sea birds is believed to have forewarned the Onges of the impending disaster and they evacuated their coastal huts and retreated to the highest point on their respective islands. If this was indeed the case, it is ironic that modern science and the supposedly sophisticated warning systems of today failed to detect the earthquake before it was too late and were well and truly trumped by 50,000 years of supposedly primitive folklore and tradition.

# BIBLIOGRAPHY

Boland, Maureen and Bridget, *Old Wives' Lore for Gardeners* (The Bodley Head, 1976)

Chamberlain, Mary, *Old Wives' Tales: The History of Remedies, Charms and Spells* (The History Press, 2012)

Crosbie, Duncan, *Tips From The Old Gardeners* (Past Times, 2002)

Hicks, Dr Rob, *Old-Fashioned Remedies: From Arsenic to Gin* (Pen and Sword, 2009)

Jack, Albert, *That's Bollocks!: Urban Legends, Conspiracy Theories and Old Wives' Tales* (Penguin, 2006)

Marr, Elspeth and Rush, Christopher (ed.) *Aunt Epp's Guide for Life* (Michael O'Mara, 2009)

Rhodes, Chloe, *One For Sorrow...: A Book of Old-Fashioned Lore* (Michael O'Mara, 2011)

# INDEX